whisky classified

whisky classified

choosing single malts by flavour

DAVID WISHART

PAVILION

To Doreen With Love

First published in Great Britain in 2002 by
PAVILION BOOKS
151 Freston Road
London
W10 6TH

An imprint of Anova Books Company Ltd

This revised edition published in 2006

Designed by Bernard Higton
Map illustrations Gill Tomblin

A CIP catalogue record for this book is available
from the British Library

ISBN 1 86205 716 8

Repro by Classicscan Pte. Ltd., Singapore
Printed in Singapore by Kyodo Printing
Company Limited

10 9 8 7 6 5 4 3 2 1

www.anovabooks.com

CONTENTS

INTRODUCTION

Many books have been written about whisky, but *Whisky Classified* was the first to compare and classify single malt whiskies by their flavour. In the first edition I introduced the "flavour profile" by which the twelve dimensions of the aroma and taste of a whisky are scored. It is an objective, scientific method of classifying and comparing single malt whiskies using sensory analysis.

This new edition takes the concept much further: firstly by covering the 94 distilleries of Scotland capable of producing malt whiskies; secondly by reviewing all the principal malt whiskies that scan the flavour spectrum; and thirdly, by introducing for the first time *Whisky Analyst,* a computer system that extends the classification to a much wider range of malt whisky expressions.

Single malt whiskies are now changing faster than ever before. In the 19th century the contraband whisky of Glenlivet, much prized at the royal court in Edinburgh, was known as "peat reek".

Malt whisky buffs might bridle at the suggestion that Speyside malts can be as peaty as the Islay style; yet heavily peated spirit is being distilled on Speyside today, as it was long ago, and lightly peated malts are being produced on Islay.

In the past 15 years, the vital infuence of the maturation cask on the flavour of malt whisky has come to the fore. Malt whisky producers are falling over themselves to bring out different "expressions" or "finishes" by using special casks or double maturation to enhance the character of their malts and increase their complexity. This new cask-centric market explores the subtle influences of the wood, the degree of peating of the barley malt, and whether the bottled malt is chill-filtered. The cask is king, and it is by far the greatest influence in the flavour of single malts in Scotland today.

Whisky Classified aims to simplify this complex subject for the newcomer to single malts, and dispels some myths along the way. They are the building blocks of the blends, the diamonds in the Crown jewels. We take each one out, dissect and examine its flavour by sensory analysis. We tell you about its history, the place where it is made, and the people who make it.

Whereas a blend is a brand recipe for a mixture of whiskies, malt and grain, the latter being produced on an industrial scale like vodka and gin, every single malt whisky has a unique provenance. When you sip a single malt whisky, you share the heart and soul of the people who made it, and you relate to those people. It connects you through time to the whisky pioneers of the 18th and 19th centuries who built the Scottish distilleries, many of which are preserved in time-honoured form to the present day. Unlike other potable spirits, all the single malt whiskies described in this book were distilled in the last millenium, and this will remain broadly true for a decade.

It is reasonable to assume that if you are reading the book then you are already interested in drinking whisky. Your first discovery may have been a single malt whisky that tasted unlike any other you had drunk before. Your next step might be to collect some diverse examples, so that you can introduce them to your friends. Later you may seek out special expressions or finishes. When you are really hooked you will probably want to visit your favourite distilleries, meet the people who make them, and sample their whiskies from Individual casks – you might buy them at cask strength, neither diluted nor chill-filtered.

The aim of this book is to help you navigate though this fascinating subject and provide some shortcuts along the way. The flavour profile was developed by analysing over a thousand tasting notes, an objective way of comparing the whiskies' distinctive and compelling flavour characteristics. The same approach is instinctively used by the Maltmaster when choosing casks for a single malt, and by the Master Blender when selecting whiskies for blending. The flavour profiles in this book offer sufficient guidance at a glance for the average malt whisky drinker, and much help for the newcomer.

Lastly, malt whiskies that are broadly similar in terms of their flavour are classified together. When you have found one that you like, experiment with other malt whiskies from the same flavour group. This book will help you assemble a collection of single malts that span the malt whisky flavour spectrum. You will then be ready to host your own malt whisky tastings with friends, to compare and contrast their flavours, their differences, where they come from, who makes them, and how they are made. *Whisky Analyst* can also extend your knowledge of rare malts and special expressions.

I invite you to share in Scotland's wonderful whisky heritage, to broaden your experience of our great malt whiskies, and to learn about the people who made them and how they were made. Always remember that the whisky you drink today was hand-crafted and laid down a decade or more before, by dedicated people confident in the knowledge that the fruits of their labour would be apprciated by generations to come. I hope you will enjoy the journey.

Slàinte mhath

David Wishart
School of Management
University of St Andrews

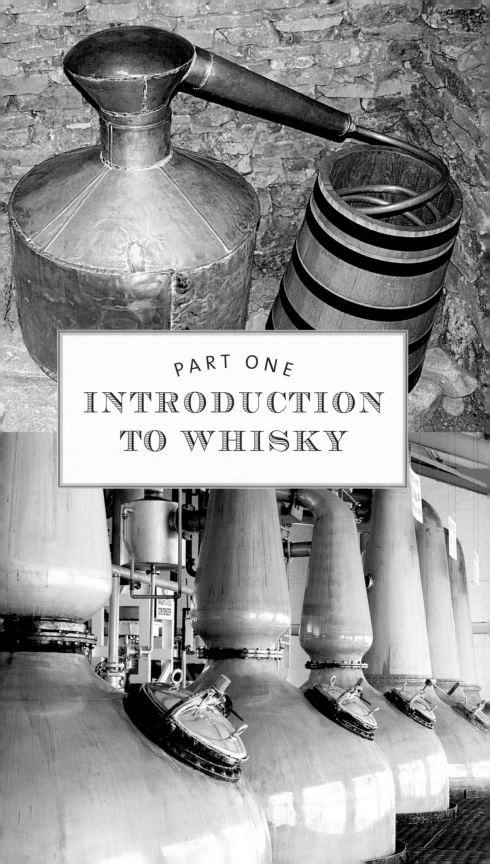

PART ONE
INTRODUCTION TO WHISKY

HISTORY OF WHISKY

The process of distillation was probably discovered by the Egyptians and Chinese for the extraction of perfumes, and adapted by monks in Europe around the eleventh century for the distillation of wine to produce brandy. The practice spread rapidly as the hedonistic effects of *aqua vitae,* "the water of life", became known. In more northern climes, unsuitable for growing grapes, the process was adapted for distilling fermented cereals, especially barley. A form of whisky was being distilled in Ireland by the twelfth century, and the practice was probably introduced to Scotland by Irish monks.

We know that St Columba travelled from Ireland and landed on Iona in AD 563, an important date in Scotland's religious history. The Scottish island of Islay, close to Iona, has a long tradition of producing malt whisky and strong historical connections with Ireland through the common language of Gaelic. Its western tip is roughly equidistant from the Giant's Causeway in Co. Antrim and Kintyre on the Scottish mainland, so it would have been a simple matter to transport a primitive still to Islay by boat. Legend has it that an Irish giant jumped to Scotland with a cask of whisky on his back, and it is no coincidence that *aqua vitae* translates into the Gaelic "uisge beatha" (pronounced ooshgy-bay) in Scots and "usque baugh" in Irish. Some argue, however, that the Gaelic term came first, and was Latinised by the monks.

The first recorded reference to whisky is in the Exchequer Rolls of Scotland for 1494, which lists an order from King James IV for "eight bolls of malt to Friar John Cor of Lindores Abbey, with which to make *aqua vitae*". Following the dissolution of the monasteries in the 16th century, many monks put their skills to work as distillers of "uisge beatha", which was famous for its medicinal qualities. James Hogg, the Ettrick Shepherd, is reported to have said "If a body could find out the exac' proper proportion and quantity that ought to be drunk every day, and keep to that, I verily trow that he might leeve for ever, without dying at a', and that doctors and kirkyards would go oot o' fashion".

Although the task of distillation was initially performed by monks, farmers were quick to acquire the new skills since it was, after all, their cereals that provided the principal ingredient and they doubtless enjoyed the product of their labours. By the 16th century, whisky distillation had become commonplace on farms

Of the Art of Distillation.

A hot Still.

A, Sheweth the bottome which ought to be of Copper.
B, The Head.
C, The barrel filled with cold water to refrigerate and condensate the water and oyl that run through the pipe or worm that is put through it.
D, A pipe of brass or pewter, or rather a worm of Tin running through the barrel.
E, The Alembick set in the furnace with the fire under it.

Early design for a primitive whisky still, including worm condenser.

The Highland Whisky Still *by Sir Edwin Landseer, 1829, depicts equipment used in illicit distillation.*

throughout Scotland, and the process was refined by the development of the familiar pear-shaped pot still and the use of cold stream water for improved condensation of the spirit. It was in the 16th century that Scots Law first interfered with whisky production. In 1505 the Guild of Surgeon Barbers in Edinburgh, now the Royal College of Physicians, was granted a monopoly for the production of *aqua vitae* for use as a medicine. By the mid-16th century prosecutions for infringement of their licence were commonplace, as whisky had become a popular drink. The first tax on spirits was imposed in 1644, and commercial distillers were operating by the end of the 17th century.

Demand increased in the 18th century, especially when the Gin Act of 1736 imposed a tax on gin which did not apply to whisky. The official production of *aqua vitae* in Scotland rose from 100,000 gallons in 1708 to 275,000 gallons in 1738. It was at about this time that the term "uisge beatha" became corrupted, first to "uiskie", then to "usky", and finally to "whisky".

It was commonplace in the 18th century for farms and large houses in Scotland to have their own still, which could legally be used to distil whisky for private consumption. Tenants of farms started full-time distillation, using portable stills of around 10 gallons, capacity. Whisky was made in the hollowed out banks of burns, on hillsides, in bothies, temporary huts and caves, even in secret rooms inside houses. In 1779 the size of private stills was reduced from 10 to 2 gallons, and Excise officers were empowered to confiscate and destroy larger stills. Two years later, private distillation was prohibited altogether, driving illicit distillers underground and more firmly establishing the commercial producers.

Queen Victoria with her gillie John Brown, at Balmoral. Their relationship aroused much speculation and inspired the film Mrs Brown.

The Wash Act of 1784 set lower Excise duty rates north of the "Highland Line" to encourage the illicit Highland distillers to become licensed. They were limited to one still of up to 20 gallons, and taxed at £1 per gallon of capacity a year. This encouraged a rapid growth of licensed distillers in the Highlands, and a further Act in 1785 prohibited the export of Highland whisky. This resulted in a massive growth in licensed distilleries in the Lowlands which, despite paying higher duty, had the advantage of exclusively selling their whiskies in the Scottish cities and in England.

In 1822, King George IV visited Edinburgh to attend a gala reception organized by Sir Walter Scott. The King declared a contraband malt whisky called "Glenlivet" to be his favourite whisky and decreed that it be used for the loyal toast.

Such was the demand for Glenlivet that extra supplies were urgently requisitioned from the Highlands. Elizabeth Grant, writing in her *Diary of a Highland Lady*, describes the Glenlivet that she sent to Holyrood as "whisky long in the wood ... mild as milk, and with the true contraband goût in it". This seems to be the earliest reference to the beneficial effects of maturing whisky in casks. It also reveals the disctintion in flavour between Highland (ie contraband) and Lowland whisky. However, maturing whisky in casks was definitely an upper-class practice, as the bulk of "uisge beatha" continued to be drunk straight from the still. Much of it must have been foul, for it was common to add honey, herbs and spices to make it palatable and to drink it in fruit punches and hot toddies.

The royal romance with whisky continued through the next two generations, with Royal Brackla distillery being granted the first royal warrant in 1835 by William IV, who proclaimed it to be his favourite whisky. In 1848, the young Queen Victoria and Prince Albert toured Scotland. They visited many towns and villages and acquired a taste for all things Scottish, including whisky. Balmoral Castle became their summer residence, and so it has remained for most of the royal family that have followed, including Queen Elizabeth II. At the start of Queen Victoria's hunts at Royal Deeside, each guest would be given a bottle of whisky and whatever remained in it at the end of the day became the perquisite of his stalker. Queen Victoria made a general order that royal coaches should always travel with a bottle of whisky under the coachman's seat, for use in emergencies. Her patronage of distilleries was recognised by the award of royal warrants to Lochnagar and Brackla.

The whisky industry flourished during Queen Victoria's reign, partly due to all things Scottish becoming popular in royal society. It was also helped by a Phylloxera plague in 1863, which devastated the vineyards of France and led English wine and brandy drinkers to turn to whisky. The quality and consistency of the whisky was unreliable, however, and it was possibly for this reason that the practice of blending was introduced. John Dewar and Arthur Bell, rival wine and spirit merchants of Perth, discovered that a more consistent product could be produced by blending several malt whiskies from different distilleries, and

their whisky blends were launched in the 1850s. This was perhaps the first time that malt whiskies were classified by their flavour, the blender's art being to select a malt, or substitute one for another, according to its flavour and thereby maintain the balance and consistency of the brand.

At about the same time, a merchant called Andrew Usher hit on the idea of introducing grain whiskies to a blend. These are distilled from unmalted barley, wheat or maize, they are lighter than malts and are cheaper to produce using the continuous patent still that had been invented by Robert Stein in 1830 and improved by Aeneas Coffey, a former Exciseman. Other blenders followed, and by the 1890s the industry was booming with new proprietary brands introduced by W.P. Lowrie, Charles Mackinlay, John Haig, John Walker, James Whyte and Charles Mackay, William Teacher, the Chivas brothers and James Buchanan, all of whom went on to become household names. So successful were they that they engaged foreign agents and began marketing their brands internationally. The most famous instance of this was Tommy Dewar's world tour of 1891–3, which resulted in 32 new agencies for Dewar's brands. As a result of this boom, existing distilleries expanded and many new ones were built. In the 1890s alone, 33 new distilleries were built, 21 of which were on Speyside. In 1885 Campbeltown had 7 distilleries, but by 1899 it had 30. Stock in warehouses also increased massively, from 2 million gallons in 1892 to 90 million gallons by 1898. However, the whisky boom was not to last beyond the beginning of the 20th century.

The first shock was the bankruptcy in 1898 of a firm of blenders run by

Above: *Whisky barrels at Wick waiting to be shipped*

Below: *Lloyd George imposed punishing taxes on Scotch whisky.*

Robert and Walter Pattison. Aside from fraudulent accounting practices, the Pattisons had also resorted to selling grain whisky that contained colouring and very little else as their "Finest Glenlivet" blend. Pattisons collapsed, causing a slump in whisky prices and stock valuations and the Pattison brothers were tried for fraud and sent to prison. Demand for whisky also fell, due in part to the Boer War which interrupted overseas trade, but also because of a general economic decline.

King Edward VII rejected whisky in favour of French wine and brandy, and fashions changed. War broke out between the whisky blenders and

distillers as to what constituted *real* whisky. In 1905, Islington Borough Council successfully prosecuted two merchants for selling whisky "not of the nature, substance and quality demanded". That judgement went to appeal, and was eventually settled by the Immature Spirit Act of 1915, which specified that whisky had to be matured in casks for a minimum of three years. This rule remains in force today – a legislative shackle on the whisky industry that does not apply to any other potable spirits. The 1915 Act was promoted by David Lloyd George, the teetotal Chancellor of the Exchequer, who declared drink to be a deadlier enemy in World War I than Germany and Austria. He substantially increased the distillers' licence fee and the duty payable on whisky. This was designed to switch consumption from whisky to beer, a policy that infuriated the Scotch whisky industry.

Distilleries were closed during World War I to preserve barley stocks for food, whisky exports were banned in 1917, and whisky duty was doubled in 1918 to increase war revenues. After the war, the distillers hoped to rebuild the industry, but were frustrated by a further increase in duty in the Budget of 1919. In the 1920s, the temperance movement gained sway in Britain, and the United States banned whisky imports and introduced prohibition.

Fortunately, US prohibition proved rather less effective than the temperance movement at suppressing whisky. Supplies of "Cutty Sark", a light, premium blend of whisky named after the fastest sailing ship of its day, were diverted to the US in the 1920s by Captain William McCoy, a bootlegger based in the Bahamas. Such was the popularity of his contraband whisky that speakeasy patrons demanded the "real McCoy", an expression for "Cutty Sark" that subsequently entered the language on both sides of the Atlantic. Whisky was also legally imported into the US as medicine, "Laphroaig" and the blend "White Horse" being prescribed for medicinal purposes by American doctors during prohibition.

By 1924, there were only 84 distilleries in production, compared to 161 in 1899, but this was to fall further, reaching a nadir in 1933 when only two malt whisky distilleries were operating. Production of whisky stopped again during World War II, and by 1945 the Scotch whisky industry had suffered 45

Captain William McCoy smuggled Cutty Sark whisky into the USA during Prohibition, where it was dubbed the "real McCoy".

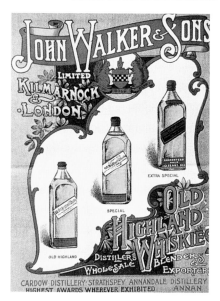

Above: An early poster for Johnnie Walker, with its distinctive square bottle first developed in the 1870s.
Below: This souvenir "sleeping" ice bucket celebrates the link between whisky and golf.

years of decline caused by three wars, US prohibition, temperance, taxation and hostile legislation. As the saying goes, things could only get better.

The 1960s was a time of construction, expansion and consolidation in the whisky industry. Many mothballed distilleries reopened, and others were rebuilt, extended or otherwise modernized. In 1958, Tormore and Glen Keith distilleries opened, the first to be built for nearly 60 years. Processes such as malting barley, maturation, blending and bottling were centralized for greater efficiency, and the marketing departments became a driving force, at least in the successful operations.

United Distillers, now Diageo, acquired a portfolio of more than 60 distilleries, though it continued to keep several in mothballs, using them only to mature other stock. Other distilleries changed hands or were absorbed into groups, several being acquired by such major companies as Pernod Ricard, Edrington Group, Bacardi and Suntory. Traditional skilled jobs, such as the stillman and maltster, were widely replaced by computerisation, mechanisation and the development of multi-skilled teams that reduced the workforce. Fearing for its independence in the face of acquisitions by the large multi-nationals, the directors of William Grant & Sons, who own Glenfiddich and Balvenie distilleries, decided in the 1960s to set aside some of their stock for sale internationally as a single malt whisky. The rest of the industry thought that the future was with blends, but fortunately Grant's were not deterred. This stroke of genius led to the revival of single malts which, throughout the 1980s and 1990s, grew in popularity. Sales of malt whiskies remain a small proportion of the total at under 15 per cent, but are growing as the market matures.

In 1975 the Scotch Malt Whisky Society was established by a group of enthusiasts, who hit upon the idea of buying individual casks collectively and bottling them for members. Membership of the Society is the goal of the connoisseur, because it gives the opportunity to experience the widest range of malt whisky flavours, from the idiosyncratic to the greats – the Society has always put much effort into tasting and selecting really great malt whiskies by their flavour.

WHISKY REGIONS

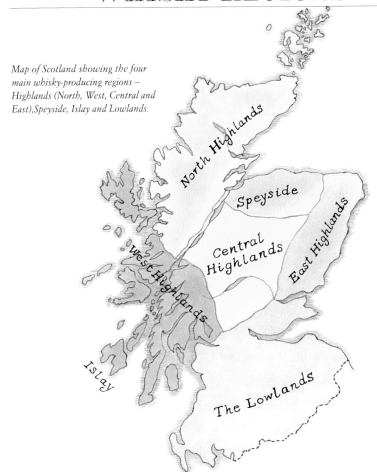

Map of Scotland showing the four main whisky-producing regions – Highlands (North, West, Central and East), Speyside, Islay and Lowlands.

The Scotch Whisky Association is the official trade organisation for the whisky industry, responsible for representing it on national and international policy issues – for example, in policing the use of the term "Scotch" and in marketing. It categorises distilleries according to four main whisky-producing regions in Scotland – Highlands, Lowlands, Islay and Speyside. This geographical split is difficult to justify today based on the number of distilleries now operating in each region: Highlands (33), Lowlands (3), Islay (8) and Speyside (50). Thus, whereas Islay is understandably singled out as a separate region, having seven operational distilleries, another six distilleries operating on other islands are classed within the Highland region, including Jura, which is closer to Islay than it is to the mainland.

The principal reason for this is that in the period 1784–1816, different Excise duty rates applied north and south of the "Highland Line". Campbeltown, which once had a thriving whisky industry of more than 32 distilleries, was officially excluded from the Highlands in 1785 and many of the producers were driven underground. Today there are only three distilleries

17

Cutting peat from an Islay moor.

operating in Campbeltown, namely Springbank, Glengyle and Glen Scotia.

There is a tradition of describing some whiskies as typically "Islay", "Highland", "Lowland" or "Speyside", and in some instances singling out particular malts as, for example, a "benchmark" or "definitive" Speyside, suggesting that malt whiskies can be differentiated by their geography. Speyside has the largest concentration of whisky distilleries in Scotland, due historically to the suitability of their isolated locations for illicit operation

and for the quality of the water. Most draw their water from the surrounding mountain springs that feed the River Spey. The mountains are covered in peat and heather, lying thinly on granite and quartz. The rain falling on these hard crystalline rocks runs quickly to the distilleries and during the winter months it is very cold. The rainwater does not pick up minerals from such rocks and is typically soft, though peaty and acidic from passing through the heather peat. It is said that the best water for whisky is soft and flows through peat over granite, which exactly describes the Spey valley topology. The combination of suitable water sources, plentiful peat for the kilns and good supplies of local barley, naturally led to the establishment of the Speyside distilleries and influenced the character of their whiskies.

Nowadays, the water source is the main feature of a distillery that is

The Spey valley is home to the largest concentration of Scotch whisky disilleries.

A view of Islay, home to seven distilleries.

believed to affect the flavour of the whisky, and even this is changing under EU regulations governing the purity of water in food and drink. With the introduction of coal and coke in the 19th century, and electric, gas and oil-fired kilns in the 20th century, the dependence on peat-fired kilns to dry the barley diminished. Distillers were able to experiment with lighter peating, and indeed many have adapted their malts to a lighter, less peated style – examples are Bunnahabhain, Jura and Tobermory; while Clynelish, Springbank and Lagavulin have reduced the level of peat phenols in their malts in recent years. Also, most distillers now obtain their malted barley from commercial maltings, rather than malting it themselves in the traditional way, and most bottle their whiskies centrally, using a different water source from that of the distillery. The use of wooden washbacks (see page 21) has given way to stainless steel ones, though many

distilleries continue to use larch or pine washbacks in an effort to preserve the original character of their whisky. Cask maturation also plays a more important part in determining the flavour of the matured whisky, with many producers using first-fill sherry casks or special cask "finishes".

It is therefore difficult to avoid the conclusion that the geographical classification of whisky has largely lost its significance. It is really only useful if you are trying to find a distillery on the map, perhaps with a view to visiting it. The map on pages 42–3 shows about 45 distilleries that welcome visitors and facilities are detailed under each distillery's entry in the A–Z section of this book. If you are a visitor to Scotland, you should try to visit at least one distillery to soak up the ambience of an industry that has grown from the crofts to the continents, and which is unambiguously associated with the word "Scotch".

MAKING WHISKY

The ingredients of malt whisky are very simple – barley, water and yeast. Barley with a high starch content is considered best, even though newer varieties, such as *Chariot* and *Optic*, yield more alcohol. The barley should also be dry, plump and free from mould, insects and vermin infestations.

Before barley can be used, it must first be malted, a process by which the starch in the barley grains is modified to produce sugar maltose for conversion to alcohol during fermentation. The first stage is to germinate the barley by alternately steeping it in water, then aerating it, usually in three cycles lasting three days. It is relevant that the water used at commercial maltings to grow the barley is usually different from the water used at the distillery. Little rootlets and a shoot form on each barley grain which swells and becomes soft and sticky. After steeping, the barley is turned regularly to keep it cool, while the starch in the grains turns to sugar and the natural enzyme diastase is released. The traditional method of turning the "green malt" is on a malting floor, using a wooden shovel called a "shiel", and this method is still used at a handful of traditional distilleries. However, it is labour intensive and has largely been replaced by commercial maltings where the germinating barley is turned mechanically in large drums.

Germination continues for about a week, by which time the green malt is now laden with natural sugars, from which the alcohol will be produced. Germination is halted by

drying the barley over a kiln using hot air, and, where peat is used to fuel the kiln, this imparts the distinctive smoky flavour to the whisky. After about 24 hours in the kiln, the green malt has become dried malt, which is crisp and sweet.

Before the Industrial Revolution, the barley was always roasted over a peat fire, hence the location of early distilleries close to plentiful supplies of peat and water, and the whisky was referred to as "peat-reek". Gradually peat was replaced by coke, and it became possible to produce lighter whiskies. Following the introduction of electricity in the mid-20th century, some distilleries began drying their barley in hot air to produce "unpeated" whiskies. Glengoyne and Auchentoshan are examples of unpeated whiskies.

Most distilleries now obtain their malted barley from commercial maltings, where it can be prepared to

Turning the barley during germination.

order. This includes specifying the amount of peat to be used in the drying process, thereby maintaining the consistency of peaty flavours in the distillery's products. It is also possible to vary the amount of peat in different batches and thus produce a range of whiskies of varying phenol content, or degrees of peatiness.

At the distillery, the malted barley is stored in large hoppers ready for use. At the next stage the barley is cleaned in dressing machines and milled into a rough flour called grist. This grist is then mixed with hot water in a vessel called a mash tun, or with the liquor retained from previous mashings. The water dissolves the maltose sugars in the flour, and the resulting liquid called "wort" is drained off and cooled ready for fermentation. The spent grain remaining in the mash tun is usually supplied to farmers as cattle feed, and the distillers are justly proud that their waste products are recycled in this way. The wort is then fermented in large vessels called

Stoking a kiln with peat to dry the barley.

washbacks. These are traditionally made of wood, such as Oregon pine or Siberian larch, though some distilleries now use stainless steel washbacks, which are easier to clean and more hygienic. Those that use wooden washbacks do so to preserve the character of their whiskies, because the wood harbours bacteria that are believed to enhance the flavour of the resulting wash. At least one distiller that experimented with stainless steel has since reverted to wooden washbacks.

Yeast is now added to the wort and fermentation begins. This is a turbulent part of the process, as the liquid froths and large amounts of carbon dioxide are emitted. Most washbacks are fitted with a revolving froth-cutter, without which the froth would overflow and be

Filling a stainless steel mash tun with hot water.

The stillhouse at Bowmore distillery.

wasted, and in some distilleries this process is now computer-controlled.

During fermentation the yeast converts sugars in the wash into carbon dioxide and alcohol, which in turn reacts with acids from the malt to form esters and aldehydes that contribute the fruity and floral flavours to the spirit. For example, acetic acid reacts with ethanol to form ethyl acetate which smells like raspberries, and with amyl alcohol to form amyl acetate which smells like pineapples. A bacterial fermentation can also occur towards the end of the process, which reduces the acidity and adds more flavours. The scents that we associate with flowers and fruits are usually due to a combination of many different esters formed during fermentation, and over a hundred different esters have been identified in the chemical analysis of whisky.

The initial phase of fermentation is spectacular as the yeast cells multiply rapidly, causing the wash to froth and bubble violently. After about two days

it slows down and is stopped, though some producers allow it to continue for 60 hours or more to develop the 'character' of the spirit by adding the flavours from a secondary bacterial fermentation. At this point the "wash" resembles a rough beer and contains 7–9 per cent alcohol. It is then pumped to the still house, where it is distilled twice or, at a few distilleries, three times – hence the term triple distilled.

The first distillation takes place in the larger "wash" stills, where the alcohols, esters, aldehydes and acids are separated from the yeast, other impurities and most of the water. The process commences when the temperature within the wash still approaches the boiling point of water. As the fermented liquid is heated, the alcohols in the wash vaporise and rise up the still and over the neck, or "lyne arm". Traditional condensers consist of a copper coil, or "worm", immersed in a tank of cold water, while modern shell-and-tube condensers consist of a cylinder containing narrow pipes through which passes a continuous flow of cold water. Here the vapours condense into a rough, oily liquid called "low wines", containing about 17 per cent alcohol.

This is then pumped into a smaller "low wines" or spirit still, where it is further refined by a second distillation. The stillman exercises much more control in this second distillation, as only the "middle cut", or heart of the spirit, is collected. This occurs as the spirit flows through a spirit safe, introduced by the Excise in 1823 to allow the stillman to observe, assess and measure the density and quality of the flowing spirit. The strongest early spirit, called "foreshots", includes impurities and is collected and combined with the next batch of low wines for re-distillation. When the flow of spirit reaches the required strength and quality, the stillman diverts it to the "spirit receiver". This involves considerable skill, as the resulting quality of the final whisky will be determined by the stillman beginning to "cut" the spirit run for collection. Towards the end of the run, the temperature in the still rises, the spirit weakens, and various oily compounds called "feints" are vaporised. As these would spoil the flavour of the whisky and dilute it, they are collected with the foreshots to be re-distilled with the next batch of low wines. The stillman thus takes only the "middle cut" from the flow of spirit, and it is only this clear new spirit, about 60–70 per cent alcohol, that is pumped to the filling store to be cooled and filled into oak casks for maturation.

At a few distilleries there is a third

The quality of the spirit is tested in the spirit safe.

distillation, involving an intermediate still, the purpose of which is to produce a lighter whisky by removing most foreshots, feints and heavier alcohols before the final distillation in the spirit still. The size and shape of the still also contribute to the flavour of the whisky, due to the relative exposure to copper which catalyses reactions that, for example, convert aldehydes produced during fermentation into acids, alcohols and esters, and remove some undesirable feints. Smaller stills offer a greater exposure to copper and therefore encourage these reactions.

The traditional method of heating stills contributes indirectly to the exposure of their copper interiors. Stills that are heated from below by direct flame fires, quickly build up deposits of burnt protein solids on the interior and these need to be removed. This is done by "rummagers", which are heavy chains that are turned inside the stills to dislodge any burnt solids and burnish the copper. The process of rummaging increases the exposure of the wash to copper and thereby enhances the flavour of the spirit. Whereas most distilleries now heat their stills

A cooper mantains the oak casks prior to filling.

using steam coils or plates, Macallan and Glenfiddich reverted to direct flame heating after experimenting with steam, in the belief that direct flame heating and rummaging yield a better spirit.

The shape of the still is also very important to the final product, and when stills are renewed they are usually copied faithfully from the originals, including any bumps and dents, in order to maintain the character of the whisky. Tall-necked stills produce a finer, lighter spirit by causing the heavier vapours to condense before reaching the swan neck and to fall back as "reflux" to be evaporated again. Shorter stills allow more of the heavy compounds to pass over the lyne arm and therefore yield a fuller, richer spirit. Some stills incorporate a "boil ball" in the neck, which helps to partially cool the vapours so that the heavier volatiles

fall back as reflux. Wash purifiers and reflux condensers are also used for this purpose, as they condense the heavier vapours on the lyne arm, returning them as liquids to the still and thereby allowing only the lightest vapours to reach the condenser. This produces a lighter, more delicate spirit. By contrast, the spirit produced by copper worm-tub condensers is heavier because there is less contact with copper, hence less catalysis and, some might say, a whisky of greater character is obtained.

The process of maturing whisky in oak casks is relatively new, having only been introduced on a large scale from the mid-19th century. Prior to that, practically all whisky was sold straight from the still at 60–70 per cent alcohol by volume. However, it was known that when whisky is stored in barrels that had previously been used for sweet wines, sherry or port, it becomes smoother and more flavoured. This process has developed into a fine art at distilleries

such as Macallan, which matures a larger proportion of its malt whiskies in Spanish oak casks specially selected in Jerez, having previously been used to mature dry oloroso sherry for about two years.

Most malt whiskies are matured in casks that have previously been used for whisky, sherry or bourbon. In 1915, it became law in the United Kingdom for all whisky to be matured in oak casks for a minimum of three years before it can be called whisky. This is in contrast to most other spirits for which no period of maturation is required by law.

The type and size of oak cask used for maturation is very important. American oak has a tighter, harder grain than European oak and is therefore less porous. This means that there is generally less interaction between the whisky and the wood of an American oak cask, so that more of the character of the spirit is retained. Oak trees grow faster in Spain and therefore the grain is more porous. Spanish casks are usually selected from those that previously held sherry or port; in some cases they are carefully prepared with a particular sherry, such as Macallan's dry oloroso, to combine the flavours of the sherry with those of the whisky and thus add to its complexity. Sometimes they are prepared using Pedro-Ximénez Sherry, which is dark and sweet and therefore conveys more deep gold colour and sweet sherry flavour. Whiskies matured in former sherry

casks are affected early on by the sherry that has seeped into the wood, whereas it is only in later years that the wood character begins to transfer to the whisky. On the other hand, when a cask has been filled with whisky for a third or fourth time, any sherry or wood character will largely be spent, so that the flavour of the spirit will be modified to a much lesser extent. Such "refill" casks are mostly used to mature whisky that is intended for blending.

Although the casks are carefully sealed to prevent leakage, oak is porous and there is therefore a loss of about 2 per cent of the spirit each year due to evaporation. This means that in 8 years of maturation, about 15 per cent of the whisky will be lost through evaporation; and after 20 years the volume can be reduced by a third or more. This is called the "angel's share", and explains the delightful aroma of maturing spirit that emanates from the warehouses. What other industry is required by law to store its entire output for several

Stillman's testing kit – hydrometer, thermometer and sample jar.

Drawing a glass of whisky direct from the casks.

years, utilising acres of warehousing space that requires monitoring and security, during which time a significant proportion of the stock simply evaporates into the air? It is hardly surprising that whisky distillers place great emphasis on the unique qualities and flavours that are added during cask maturation, especially for those whiskies that are aged the longest.

Whisky is traditionally matured and gently mellowed in low, stone-built, earth-floored "dunnage" warehouses, where the casks are only stacked up to three high. If these warehouses are situated by the sea, the damp salty air permeates the casks, thereby imparting a salty note to the maturing whisky. Inland warehouses can have a more disruptive effect on the maturation process, due to the wider variations in temperature. It is normal for a black fungus that lives off evaporating alcohol, the *champignon ivrogne*, to grow on the walls of dunnage warehouses and even spread to the nearby trees. Look out for this on your visit to a distillery – if you do not see a blackened warehouse, this is an indication that their whiskies are being matured elsewhere. In modern warehouses, casks can be stacked twelve high, temperatures are controlled, and

there is less air circulation. This can adversely affect the maturing whisky, and many distilleries use a combination of both types of warehouse.

Some distillers have recently introduced new "finishing" or double-wood processes that impart additional flavours during the final stages of maturation. The whisky is removed from conventional casks after the normal period of 10–15 years, and transferred to newer casks that are specially prepared with a fortified wine such as sherry or port, or a spirit such as cognac or calvados. These methods were partly introduced because of the scarcity of sherry casks, and are used sparingly for the last 9–12 months of maturation.

In 1996, Glenmorangie introduced its range of special "wood finishes", utilising casks that had previously contained port, madeira or sherry; more recently, Malaga wine and Côte de Nuits Burgundy wood finishes have been added to their range. Glendronach, Glenfarclas and others have moved towards Macallan's approach, using sherry casks in their maturation. Glenfiddich "marry"

Display of sample bottles, essential for blending.

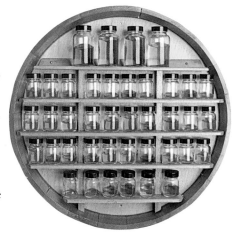

whiskies aged at least 15 years from different casks in a Solera vat to produce a sherried malt. These special cask finishes also provide a new marketing angle that is intended to make the whiskies appeal more directly to wine drinkers.

By definition, a single malt whisky originates from a "single" Scottish distillery. By its age, you know roughly when it was distilled. Sometimes the year of distillation is stated explicitly, but more usually the bottle will carry a statement such as "10 years old". This does not mean that the whisky was distilled exactly 10 years ago, because the age statement has, by law, to be the *minimum* age of the whisky in the bottle. It is quite common, for example, to marry casks of different ages which are at least 10 years old, to produce a single malt that is described as "10 years old". A key skill is cask selection, the process of marrying the contents of different casks in a large vat for several weeks or months before it is bottled. Sometimes a particularly good cask of whisky may be selected and bottled at cask strength to be sold as a special version.

Only a handful of distilleries bottle their own whiskies. Most are bottled in factories, where the whisky is reduced from cask strength to bottle strength, typically 40% alcohol by volume. The water added to reduce the whisky is usually different from the distillery's water. It is de-ionised, effectively neutral in flavour, but this is another factor that diminishes the case for the water in the

whisky being special. However, there is worse to come – when you add water or ice to your whisky before drinking it, you potentially contaminate its flavour with your local supply.

It is common in hot climes to add ice to whisky. This lowers the temperature of the whisky and, with some, a fine haze can develop. Consumers generally do not like drinking cloudy whisky – it looks bad. The producers' response was to introduce chill-filtration, by which the temperature of the whisky is reduced to around zero, causing heavy long-chain esters to precipitate, forming a haze. The whisky is then passed through a fine filter, which removes the heavy esters, before being bottled. This prevents a haze forming when the whisky is later cooled by adding ice, but it also removes some of the flavour. I advise you to try non chill-filtered whiskies and not to worry if a haze develops, but just enjoy the fuller flavour of the natural malt whisky.

A collector's edition of The Macallan, supplied in a decanter and presentation box.

WHISKY FLAVOURS

The standard malt whisky flavour profile used in this book has been developed from a wide review of hundreds of malt whisky tasting notes. Several current books on malt whisky and distillers' tasting notes were reviewed, and a vocabulary of over 400 aromatic and flavour adjectives and nouns used to describe the aroma and flavour of malt whiskies was compiled (see appendix).

The starting point for evaluating this vocabulary was the Pentlands Flavour Wheel, developed in 1979 by chemists at the Pentlands Scotch Whisky Research Institute (now the Scotch Whisky Research Institute). This was a terminology that classified the flavours and aromas found in whisky around the hub of a wheel, under 14 headings: primary taste, mouthfeel, nasal, phenolic, feints, cereal, aldehydic, estery, sweet, woody, oily, sour, sulphury and stale.

While the Pentlands Flavour Wheel provided a useful reference for the assessment of spirit by the industry, it was difficult for consumers to interpret and so it was simplified in the 1980s by John Lamond and Aberlour Distillery into the Aberlour Tasting Wheel. This concept was developed further in 1997 by MacLean, Newton and Swan into a three-tier tasting wheel. The flavours are described in everyday terms under eight "cardinal aromatic groups", namely: winey, cereal, estery, floral, peaty, feinty, sulphury and woody.

For the flavour profile in this book, a representative malt whisky from each Scottish distillery was scored according to whether or not

notes corresponding to the eight cardinal aromatic groups were present. The representative malt whisky selected was normally the distillery's most popular expression, though in some cases the choice was not straightforward. It is beyond the scope of this book to attempt to classify the entire range, though this is now possible using *Whisky Analyst* (see pages 230–33). Rather, the purpose of this book is to evaluate malt whiskies that are readily available in bars, restaurants and supermarkets today, at affordable prices.

With this aim firmly in mind, a target malt whisky, which had been aged in casks for about 10–15 years, was selected for each distillery. Even this standard is difficult to maintain because, for example, the main expressions from Lagavulin and Mortlach are matured for 16 years, while the very popular Auchentoshan Select, Glen Moray Classic and Loch Lomond malts carry no age statements. In the absence of a

Pentlands Flavour Wheel.

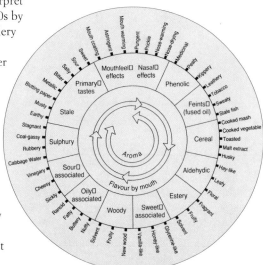

readily available 10 years old malt, the best-seller from each distillery was chosen for evaluation. It is important to note that each flavour profile in this book is for one malt whisky expression only, and cannot be extrapolated to others from the same distillery. There can be, and often are, considerable variations in the character of malts emanating from one distillery due to ageing, cask selection or special finishing.

In scoring the malts according to MacLean's eight cardinal aromatic groups, and from discussions with industry experts, it became apparent that some of the groups are too broadly constructed to reflect the diversity of different flavours found in the tasting notes. For example, the "peaty" group embraces smoky, peaty and pungent together with medicinal, iodine and seaweed notes, and whereas the former clearly derive from the use of peat to dry the barley and in the water, the latter can relate to water character or the maturation of whiskies near the sea. Although these flavours do often go together, for example as on Islay, this is more an accident of history and location than a causal link.

Likewise, sherried notes occur widely and yet MacLean's "winey" group also includes chocolate and nutty features related to the cask used in maturation. The different types and sizes of casks in which whiskies are matured give rise to a host of cask-related descriptions. For example, chocolate, nutty and vanilla are flavours derived from the type of oak used, whereas winey, port and sherried describe flavours introduced solely by the previous contents of the cask.

For the flavour profile used in this book, a separate group has, therefore, been created for smoky and peaty notes, and similarly for winey and sherried

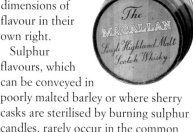

notes, because both of these are important dimensions of flavour in their own right.

Sulphur flavours, which can be conveyed in poorly malted barley or where sherry casks are sterilised by burning sulphur candles, rarely occur in the common malt whiskies on the market today. The sulphur group has, therefore, been excluded from the flavour profile. This is also true, to some extent, of the feints group, which includes undesirable flavours such as plastic, cheesy, soapy, sweaty and musty, which arise during the later stages of distillation and during maturation due to bung-cloth deterioration. Fortunately, such descriptions are rare in modern malt whiskies, thanks to the skill of the stillman when taking the middle cut, and of the Maltmaster when selecting casks for vatting. However, the "feinty" group also includes desirable flavours such as tobacco, leather, hessian and tea chests, terms that occur quite widely in the description of popular malt whiskies. They have, therefore, been incorporated in the flavour profile as a separate feature, under the heading "tobacco".

Lastly, there are liberal references in whisky literature to the sweetness (or sourness) and body of whiskies. Whether a whisky is sweet or dry is clearly a characteristic of its flavour that will determine its appeal, as with wine and other drinks. Body is more difficult, but can relate to the occasion on which a whisky might be drunk. For example, a lighter, aromatic whisky is more suitable as an aperitif, when the taste buds are fresh and receptive. By contrast, a full-bodied malt whisky with a big personality, such as a heavily-peated Islay malt, might be enjoyed as an after-dinner drink with a strong cheese to complement it.

This book's standard flavour profile, therefore, comprises 12 flavour features into which the vocabulary of over 400 malt whisky adjectives and descriptive nouns has been grouped (see page 244). It has been presented at several scientific meetings, and was circulated with industry surveys, as a result of which some final adjustments were made. The flavour profile can be summarized as shown opposite.

The initial analysis, based solely on whether flavours were present or not in whiskies, proved to be too crude. This was because whisky writers and distillers differentiate quite carefully between pronounced features, light notes and hints. Throughout this book, these 12 flavour categories are, therefore, scored on a scale of 0-4 according to the intensity with which each feature is present in a whisky. The intensity rating is set out below.

Even so whisky writers and distillers do not always agree on the intensity of the flavours they discern, so there is inevitably an element of judgment involved in determining these ratings.

This book contains a flavour profile for each single malt whisky, in the following style:

Feature	Profile
●●	Body
●●	Sweetness
●●●	Smoky
●	Medicinal
	Tobacco
●●	Honey
●	Spicy
●	Winey
●	Nutty
●●	Malty
●	Fruity
●	Floral

HIGHLAND PARK
Single Malt Scotch Whisky
Orkney Islands
AGED 12 YEARS

This is the flavour profile for Highland Park 12 years old. In this case it shows that most of the flavours are present in the whisky, but none dominates – the most distinctive characteristic is smoke, a definite note that is sometimes referred to as the malt's "signature". Otherwise, the flavour profile is well-balanced and illustrates the complexity of this highly regarded single malt whisky.

Some readers will doubtless disagree with some of the flavour profiles contained in this book. But then, this is the essence of the pleasure of drinking malt whisky – to explore, evaluate and discover the delights of the barley and the wood, and to find that elusive bottle that unifies the components of flavour in exactly the right combination for your palate or for a special occasion.

0		Not present
1	●	Low Hints
2	●●	Medium Notes
3	●●●	Definite Notes
4	●●●●	Pronounced

FLAVOUR PROFILE

Body: its weight or fullness, influenced by the size of the still and the type of cask (light, through medium, to full-bodied).

Sweetness: sugars in the wash not converted during fermentation or by catalysis during distillation, and glucose extracted from new casks during maturation (dry, through medium-sweet, to sweet).

Smoky: where peat is used in kilning, and where the water flows through peat bogs (bonfires, burnt-heather, peaty, phenolic, pungent, kippery, mossy, earthy, fishing-nets, turfy).

Medicinal: salty, iodine flavours usually associated with seashore maturation (brine, iodine, menthol, salty, sea-air, seaweed, turpentine).

Tobacco: feints introduced at distillation and during maturation, desirable in moderation (tea-chests, libraries, old-books, leather, leather-polish, car-seats, saddles, garden-sheds, hessian, musty).

Honey: released by catalysis of aldehydes during distillation or extracted from oak wood during maturation, especially new oak or bourbon casks (beeswax, heather-honey, mead, butterscotch, caramel, fudge, toffee, treacle, vanilla).

Spicy: extracted from oak wood during maturation, particularly where new wood is used (bay leaves, cedar, cinnamon, cloves, ginger, nutmeg, oaky, pepper, pine, sandalwood, tannic, woody).

Winey: flavours from what the casks contained before being filled with whisky, such as a special preparation of the cask with sherry, port or madeira to add a special finish (Chardonnay, Chenin Blanc, fino sherry, grapey, liqueurish, madeira, oloroso, port, sherry).

Nutty: mainly oak lactones extracted from casks during maturation, especially European oak, or fatty acids formed by bacterial growth during fermentation (almonds, hazelnuts, oily, walnuts, buttery, chocolate, creamy).

Malty: characteristics of the malt and yeast not removed in fermentation, usually showing in immature whiskies (barley, biscuits, cereal, grain, mashy, mealy, cooked-veg, malt-extract, husky, burnt-toffee, cake, roasted-coffee, liquorice, toasted, baking, yeasty).

Fruity: higher alcohols, aldehydes and esters formed at fermentation, by catalysis during distillation, and by reactions with oak wood during maturation (citric, estery, lemony, limey, oranges, tart, melons, peaches, pear-drops, strawberries, sweet-shop, stewed-apples, Christmas-pudding, fruit-cake, dried-fruit, raisins, sultanas, bubble-gum, solvent).

Floral: esters and aldehydes formed during fermentation and by reactions with oak wood during maturation (aromatic, fragrant, honeysuckle, perfumed violets, sugared-almonds, greenhouse, mint, sherbet, cut-barley, grassy, leafy, sappy, botanical, hay-like, heathery, herbal, meadows).

WHISKY TYPES

Once the malt whiskies have been scored on the flavour profile, they can more readily be compared. Two malt whiskies that have exactly the same flavour profile, correctly scored, can be considered to be the same or similar in terms of their flavour. Some whisky *connoisseurs* would argue that this is not the case, and that every malt whisky is unique. While this is clearly true if their features are analysed to the utmost degree of refinement, it is not necessarily very helpful. For the purposes of better understanding *types* of people, plants, animals, insects, etc, it is usually helpful to *classify* them – indeed language is a means of classifying and hence describing everything we encounter. The same is true of whisky, particularly from the consumer's point of view, as classification leads to a better understanding of how one product compares with another and, therefore, what to try next.

This, then, is an attempt to classify single malt whiskies according to their *flavour* as opposed to where they are made, or who makes them, or how they are sold. The standard flavour profile was scored for each whisky, and these profiles were then used to classify all the principle malt whiskies, using a scientific method known as "cluster analysis", originally developed in the biological sciences to describe the relationships between plants and animals. Put simply, the method groups malt whiskies that have *broadly* the same scores on all twelve flavour features, into the same clusters. The result is that all the whiskies in a cluster are similar in terms of their flavour profiles, while the clusters are differentiated by one or more of the flavour features.

In order to validate this system of classification, it was sent to all the distillers and to other industry experts in surveys and published in scientific journals. Many useful comments and some criticisms were received. Of those that replied, over 90 per cent thought that the approach was a reasonable one, yet needed further refinement. All the criticisms were carefully reviewed, in particular where respondents thought that a comparison was wrong or that certain malt whiskies were in the wrong cluster. The flavour profiles were revised in the light of these observations. The flavour profile was broadened to the present 5-point scale and additional sources of tasting notes were reviewed, including those of distillers, retailers and malt whisky clubs.

The cluster analysis was repeated on the revised scores and several different cluster levels were considered. The one that accords most closely with the industry surveys is the 10-cluster grouping shown opposite. It is the reference classification against which all

Cluster A (Full-bodied, medium-sweet, pronounced sherry with fruity, spicy, malty notes and nutty, smoky hints): Balmenach, Dailuaine, Dalmore, Glendronach, Macallan, Mortlach, Royal Lochnagar

Cluster B (Medium-bodied, medium-sweet, with nutty, malty, floral, honey and fruity notes): Aberfeldy, Aberlour, Ben Nevis, Benrinnes, Benromach, Blair Athol, Cragganmore, Edradour, Glencadam, Glenfarclas, Glenturret, Knockando, Longmorn, Scapa, Strathisla

Cluster C (Medium-bodied, medium-sweet; fruity, floral, honey, malty notes and spicy hints): Balvenie, Benriach, Clynelish, Dalwhinnie, Glendullan, Glen Elgin, Glen Ord, Glenlivet, Linkwood, Royal Brackla

Cluster D (Light, medium-sweet, low or no peat, with fruity, floral, malty notes and nutty hints): An Cnoc, Isle of Arran, Auchentoshan, Aultmore, Cardhu, Glengoyne, Glen Grant, Glentauchers, Mannochmore, Speyside, Tamdhu, Tobermory

Cluster E (Light, medium-sweet, low peat, with floral, malty notes and fruity, spicy, honey hints): Allt á Bhainne, Bladnoch, Braeval, Bunnahabhain, Caperdonich, Glenallachie, Glenburgie, Glenkinchie, Glenlossie, Glen Moray, Inchgower, Loch Lomond, Tomintoul

Cluster F (Medium-bodied, medium-sweet, low peat; malty notes and sherry, honey, spicy hints): Ardmore, Auchroisk, Deanston, Glen Deveron, Glen Keith, Glenrothes, Fettercairn, Tomatin, Tormore, Tullibardine

Cluster G (Medium-bodied, sweet, low peat and floral notes): Dufftown, Glenfiddich, Glen Spey, Miltonduff, Speyburn

Cluster H (Medium-bodied, medium-sweet, with smoky, fruity, spicy notes and floral, nutty hints): Balblair, Craigellachie, Glen Garioch, Glenmorangie, Oban, Old Pulteney, Strathmill, Tamnavulin, Teaninich

Cluster I (Medium-light, dry, with smoky, spicy, honey notes and nutty, floral hints): Bowmore, Bruichladdich, Glen Scotia, Highland Park, Isle of Jura, Springbank

Cluster J (Full-bodied, dry, pungent, peaty and medicinal, with spicy, tobacco notes): Ardbeg, Caol Ila, Lagavulin, Laphroaig, Talisker

malt whiskies are now classifed using *Whisky Analyst*. Readers who are familiar with malt whiskies may recognize the two extremes of strongly sherried malts (Cluster A) and the heavily peated, mainly Islay malts (Cluster J). Adjacent to these polar benchmarks are the lightly sherried (clusters B and C) and lightly peated (clusters H and I) malts, with the light-bodied, floral and malty clusters, including four largely unpeated groups (clusters D–G) falling in the middle.

The 10 clusters can be combined into broader groupings (see below), which can be helpful when selecting 6 or 4 sample whiskies for tasting. The cluster of pungent, peaty Islay malts (J) is most distinctive, being maintained as a separate group to the end of the analysis, with the "sherries" of clusters A–C the next most distinctive, and clusters H–I separated as a group of well-balanced malts showing more complexity with no dominant features.

10 CLUSTERS

Cluster	Sample whiskies
A	Mortlach
B	Strathisla
C	Glenlivet
D	Auchentoshan
E	Glenkinchie
F	Tomatin
G	Arran
H	Oban
I	Bowmore
J	Lagavulin

6 CLUSTERS

Cluster	Sample whiskies
A	Dalmore
B C	Glenfarclas Dalwhinnie
D E	Glen Grant Glen Moray
F G	Deanston Speyburn
H I	Old Pulteney Springbank
J	Ardbeg

4 CLUSTERS

Cluster	Sample whiskies
A B C	Macallan Aberlour Balvenie
D E F G	Glengoyne Bunnahabhain Glenrothes Glenfiddich
H I	Glenmorangie Highland Park
J	Laphroaig

TASTING WHISKY

It is a curious fact that when we taste whisky we use our nose far more than our mouth or tongue. Taste is a combination of the primary impression on the tongue supplemented by aromas detected by the nose, the nose being far more sensitive than the tongue. It has been estimated that for every taste bud on the tongue there are 10,000 taste receptors in the nose. That is why master blenders 'nose' their whiskies rather than taste them, and when they are working they seldom drink any whisky at all.

While it can be instructive to evaluate whiskies simply by nosing them, for those of us who enjoy drinking whisky this is not exactly fun. But it can be a good discipline to begin a tasting session by pouring 5 or 6 malt whiskies into separate glasses and nosing them all before starting to drink any of them. The issue of what whiskies to choose for a tasting and the order in which they should be nosed and tasted is discussed later.

First, select the correct type of glass. The standard cut-glass whisky tumbler is not the ideal shape for nosing whiskies. The nosing glass used in the whisky industry is tulip shaped like a sherry glass with a narrow mouth and has graduations marked on the side. The narrow mouth is important for containing the aroma that rises from the whisky, so that when we nose it we get the maximum fragrance. For the same reason it is helpful to cover the mouth of the glass with a watch glass cover or lid that prevents the aromas from escaping, but it would be pedantic to regard these as essential. In the absence of proper nosing glasses, use small, tulip shaped wine glasses.

The next issue is the strength of the whisky to nose and taste, for it will be evident that not all malt whiskies are supplied at the same alcoholic strength. Although the majority are bottled at 40%, others are 43%, 46% and cask strength 55–60%.

In order to make a fair comparison between different whiskies, they should be nosed at the same alcoholic strength, and the industry standard is 20% alcohol by volume. This may not be popular with those who do not approve of adding water to their whisky. It is, however, an accepted fact that our taste receptors work best when not anaesthetised by alcohol, and 20% is a good strength at which the esters are fully released and can be most easily detected. Some people add much more water than whisky, and this is also a good discipline especially if there is a need to remain sober. It is common in the West of Scotland to add lemonade to whisky and in America and other hot climes to add ice, but these and other mixers are not recommended for malt whiskies because they modify the flavour.

For a nosing session, it is good practice to nose at full strength first and note any initial impressions. If you inhale too strongly, you may feel nose prickle – this is caused by the alcohol vapour temporarily overloading your senses. When this happens, wait a moment and draw the whisky's aroma gently into your nose, trying to identify the individual fragrances. Next add enough still, soft spring water to reduce the whisky to 20% and nose again. Standard nosing glasses have two graduations on the side, the lower one being the level to fill with whisky and the upper one being the level to top up with water. They correspond to equal volumes, and hence assume that the whisky has been bottled at 40%, so a slight adjustment is needed for a stronger whisky.

To taste the whisky, take a generous sip and note the body and mouth feel – is it smooth, creamy, oily or spirity? Move the whisky around your mouth checking the balance of sweet, sour, salty and bitter sensations detected by your tongue. Continue to check for fragrances through your nose, and estimate the strength of each flavour you detect using the flavour profile as a guide. As you swallow, note how long the flavours linger and what you taste after the whisky is gone – a long finish is considered desirable by connoisseurs.

Many people when starting to drink malt whiskies prefer light, aperitif styles, whereas experienced whisky drinkers are looking for depth, balance and complexity. Those who feel the urge to express their judgements by awarding marks-out-of-ten for quality are usually seeking balance, complexity and length, and their preferences do not necessarily coincide with those of beginners. A balanced whisky lacks any pronounced or dominating flavours, but presents a combination that often appears sequentially like peeling away the layers of an onion. This is why whisky writers usually describe the colour, nose, palate and finish in that order, which is the normal sequence in which a whisky is enjoyed.

We are now ready to start using the flavour profile to plan a tutored whisky tasting that illustrates the full variation in whisky styles. The first problem is that whereas the bottles usually need to be presented in line, the variations in flavour are far more complex than linear. The simplest model is two-dimensional, by which the degree of peat is represented in one direction and the degree of sherry or wine in another. It may be useful to select reference malts, such as the unpeated Glengoyne, the heavily peated Laphroaig and the strongly sherried Macallan. Most of the other malt whiskies fall somewhere between these poles (in the chart), such as Highland Park (above). If the chart is now flattened into one dimension, the best representation places the lightest malt whiskies in the centre and work out to the polar extremes of cluster A to the left and cluster J to the right. When I host a *Whisky Classified* tutored tasting, I normally select six malt whiskies in this arrangement, such as those

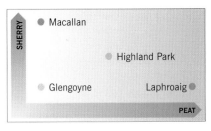

illustrated in the table below. They are normally arranged in line, but if space permits they can be placed on a square table in the centre of the room, arranged as in the chart below. The whiskies at the centre are those with the lightest flavours, least modified by peating of the malted barley or maturation in European sherry casks. In a very broad sense, they allow the character of the spirit to show through, and should be tasted first. The tasting usually proceeds to the whiskies on the

A	B – C	D – E	F – G	H – I	J
Dalmore	Aberlour	Auchentoshan	Deanston	Bowmore	Ardbeg
Glendronach	Balvenie	Bunnahabhain	Glenfiddich	Glenmorangie	Lagavulin
Macallan	Glenfarclas	Glengoyne	Glenrothes	Highland Park	Laphroaig
Mortlach	Strathisla	Glenkinchie	Speyburn	Springbank	Talisker

left, which have been more influenced by the choice of cask for maturation, and concludes with those to the right, which have been more influenced by the use of peat.

It can be noted that this is the reverse of chronological order, since the degree of peating of the barley is always the first decision, followed by mashing of the grist when peaty water can be introduced. Fermentation and distillation are next, when the character of the spirit is determined by the production processes used and the middle cut is taken. Maturation is the final stage, when cask selection is crucial to the texture and flavour, in some cases modified by special finishing. However, in guiding a tutored tasting there is no escaping the fact that cluster J should be tasted last, because these whiskies have the strongest peaty flavours and would spoil the palate for the more subtly flavoured malts in the centre. In conclusion, the whiskies in clusters B–C and H–I are those that frequently do well in tasting competitions, because they display balance and complexity with no particular flavours dominating.

Now that you have explored the delights and complexities of malt whisky, it is time to raise your glass and toast the people who made it. Making malt whisky is both an art and a science. There is a lot of science in whisky making, from the maltster's role in ensuring the quality of the malted barley, the mashman's control of mashing and fermentation, the stillman's control of the distillation, and the Maltmaster's selection of casks

for filling. It's a team effort to craft a malt whisky, and when you drink it you share their soul and skill. They are all vital to the quality of the final product.

It is also a commitment by them to the future, for the whisky produced today may not be drunk for a generation. It will lie quietly maturing in the cask for at least ten years before it is bottled and reaches you, by which time a new team may be working the distillery. It is thus a promise from one generation to the next, that the product of their labours past will be worthy of your future toast.

The most dramatic moment in the whole process, and one that is crucial to the quality and character of the whisky, is when the stillman takes the middle cut. Whisky production at most distilleries continues around the clock, therefore this is as likely to occur in the middle of the night as in a normal working day. So, I invite you to raise your glass and toast the stillman as he pursues his lonely craft on the night shift, in the certain knowledge that it will take a decade or more before the new spirit emerges from the cask as single malt whisky for us to enjoy.

Scotia's Gold

Raise a glass to the stillman's skill,
    alone in the night, he tends his still.
Charges the wash, brings to the boil,
    dewy beads form in a copper coil.

Starts at a trickle, then a flow,
    cloudy foreshots the first to show.
Checks for strength, clear of mist,
    crystal spirit o' coarse milled grist.

Spirit safe cranks, sounding the hour,
    seizes the essence o' barley flower.
Clear flows the run, pulses the heart,
    cuts the middle wi' his stillman's art.

Draught o' his craft, now bares its soul,
    character's formed in a tulip bowl.
Then raise your glass, my kindred host,
    wi' Scotia's gold, our worthy toast.

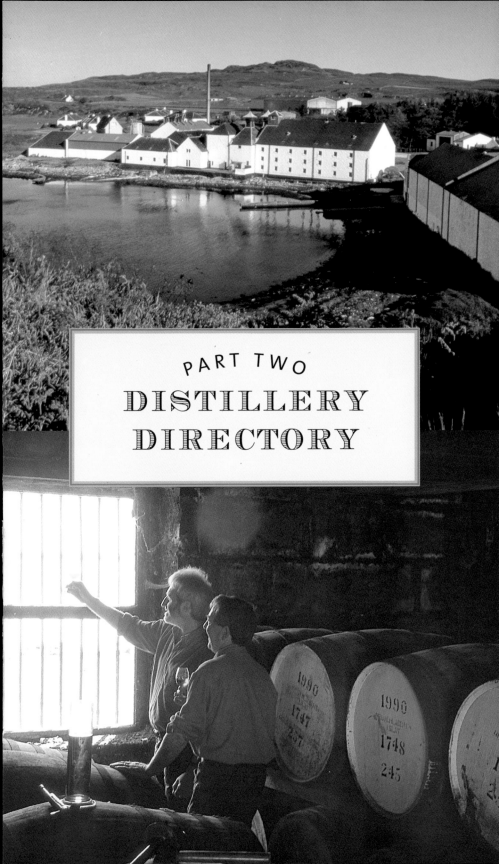

PART TWO

DISTILLERY DIRECTORY

MAP OF DISTILLERIES

1 Highland Park
2 Scapa
3 Pulteney
4 Clynelish
5 Glenmorangie
6 Balblair
7 Teaninich
8 Dalmore
9 Glen Ord
10 Glen Moray
11 Miltonduff
12 Glenlossie
13 Mannochmore
14 Linkwood
15 Longmorn
16 Benriach
17 Glen Elgin
18 Speyburn
19 Glen Grant
20 Glenrothes
21 Glen Spey
22 Macallan
23 Cardhu
24 Tamdhu
25 Knockando
26 Craigellachie
27 Balvenie
28 Glenfiddich
29 Glendullan
30 Mortlach
31 Dufftown
32 Aberlour
33 Glenallachie
34 Benrinnes

35 Glenfarclas
36 Tormore
37 Cragganmore
38 Dailuaine
39 Glenlivet
40 Tamnavulin
41 Tomintoul
42 Balmenach
43 Speyside
44 Tomatin
45 Royal Brackla
46 Inchgower
47 Macduff (Glen Deveron)
48 Aultmore
49 Strathisla
50 Strathmill
51 Glen Keith
52 Knockdhu (An Cnoc)
53 Glendronach
54 Ardmore
55 Auchroisk
56 Benromach
57 Glen Garioch
58 Royal Lochnagar
59 Fettercairn
60 Blair Athol
61 Edradour
62 Aberfeldy
63 Glenturret
64 Tullibardine
65 Deanston
66 Glengoyne

67 Loch Lomond
68 Oban
69 Ben Nevis
70 Dalwhinnie
71 Tobermory
72 Talisker
73 Bunnahabhain
74 Bruichladdich
75 Bowmore
76 Caol Ila
77 Isle of Jura
78 Laphroaig
79 Lagavulin
80 Ardbeg

81 Glen Scotia
82 Springbank
83 Isle of Arran
84 Auchentoshan
85 Glenkinchie
86 Bladnoch
87 Kilchoman
88 Glenburgie
89 Caperdonich
90 Glentauchers
91 Allt-a-Bhainne
92 Braeval
93 Glencadam
94 Blackwood

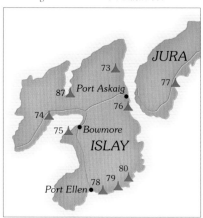

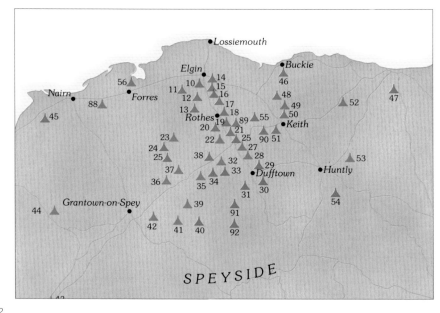

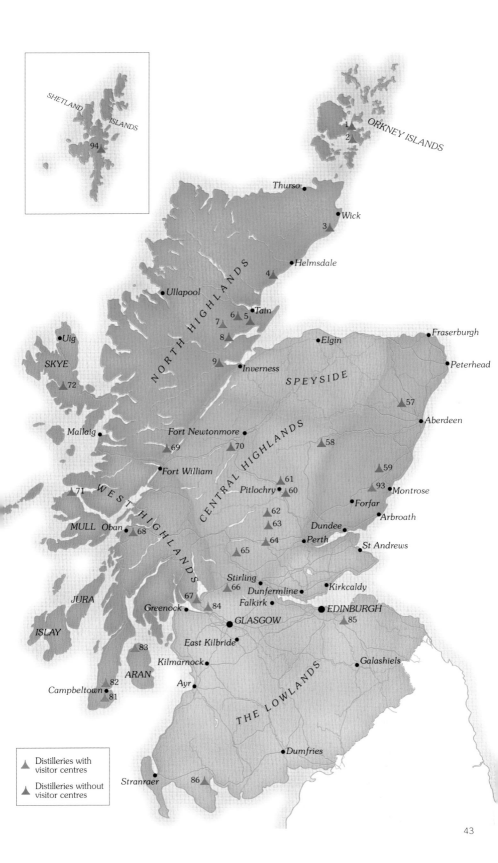

SHETLAND ISLANDS

94

ORKNEY ISLANDS

1
2

Thurso

Wick

3

Helmsdale

4

Ullapool

NORTH HIGHLANDS

Tain

7 6 5
8

Elgin

Fraserburgh

Peterhead

Uig

SKYE

72

9

Inverness

SPEYSIDE

57

Aberdeen

Mallaig

Fort Newtonmore

CENTRAL HIGHLANDS

58

69 70

Fort William

59

71

WEST HIGHLANDS

Pitlochry

61
60

93 Montrose

62

Forfar

Arbroath

MULL Oban

68

63

64

Dundee

Perth

St Andrews

65

Stirling

66

Dunfermline

Kirkcaldy

67

84

Falkirk

Greenock

GLASGOW

EDINBURGH

85

JURA

East Kilbride

83

Kilmarnock

Galashiels

ISLAY

ARAN

Ayr

82

Campbeltown

81

THE LOWLANDS

Dumfries

▲ Distilleries with
   visitor centres

▲ Distilleries without
   visitor centres

Stranraer

86

43

ABERFELDY

{*aber*-FELL-*dee*}

The site of Aberfeldy distillery was chosen for its proximity to a good water supply and the Victorian railway line to Perth. It was built in 1896 by Tommy Dewar, the younger son of John Dewar, who founded Dewar & Sons of Perth. Beside the distillery is an original 1939 Barclays steam locomotive – the *Dailuaine No. 1* – that delivered coal and grain and left loaded with casks of matured whisky. The label on the bottle features the founder, John Dewar, and the distillery as it was in the nineteenth century.

Aberfeldy's original late-Victorian buildings are spoiled somewhat by a 1970s still-house extension. However, the original floor maltings have been sensitively converted to a fine visitor centre, "Dewar's World of Whisky", which recounts the history of the Dewar family, company and world-famous White Label blends.

The water source is Pitilie Burn, which flows from springs that originally supplied Pitilie distillery in the mid-nineteenth century. Scottish barley is now malted to order and dried using a moderate amount of peat. The distillery operates a computer-controlled stainless steel mash tun, 8 Siberian larch washbacks, and 4 large, bulbous pot stills. The wash is fermented for about 48 hours, using a mix of distillery and brewers' yeast, and carbon dioxide is extracted from the washbacks by fans. Aberfeldy was sold with the Dewar's portfolio to Bacardi in 1998, hence its malt whisky was distilled by the previous owners. The whisky is matured in Spanish and American oak casks.

Aberfeldy malt whisky is available at 12 years old, as featured, a special 1980 vintage cask strength, and as a 25 years old edition. It is the signature malt in Dewar's White Label blend, which has been America's best-selling Scotch whisky for over a century. Other bottlings of Aberfeldy malt whisky are available from Adelphi and Gordon & MacPhail.

The "World of Whisky" visitor centre is excellent. It follows the story of the House of Dewar, started by John Dewar with a modest wine and spirit shop in Perth in 1846, and built by his sons and successors into an international company now selling in over 200 countries. There is a triple screen audio-visual presentation in a comfortable auditorium and personal audio handsets, with a commentary in five languages. There is also a fine exhibition with various interactive games and challenges to test the visitor's knowledge of whisky.

A guided tour of Aberfeldy distillery is included in the admission price, and exclusive bottles, gifts and souvenirs can be purchased in the Brand Store. The visitor centre is open all year and offers light refreshments, as well as a free dram of Dewar's White Label. There is a nature trail beside the burn, where lucky visitors may spot one of the rare red squirrels, and there are many places of interest in and around Aberfeldy.

Feature	Profile
●●	Body
●●	Sweetness
●●	Smoky
	Medicinal
	Tobacco
●●	Honey
●	Spicy
●●	Winey
●●	Nutty
●●	Malty
●●	Fruity
●●	Floral

Age 12 years
Strength 40%
Nose Fragrant, citric zest aroma, with light smoke, honey and spice discernible
Taste Fresh, fruity and malty, medium-sweet with floral, oak and honey notes
Cluster B Medium-bodied, medium-sweet, with nutty, malty, floral, honey and fruity notes
Similar to Blair Athol, Benromach, Scapa

45

ABERLOUR

{*aber*-LOW-*er*}

Aberlour is Gaelic for the "mouth of the chattering burn". It is an ancient and beautiful place, probably founded by Druids, as there has been a community here for more than 1400 years. There is evidence of its long heritage all around, from the age-old oak trees above Linn Falls to the mysterious standing stones on Fairy Hill.

The distillery is located in the heart of Aberlour village, on the banks of the Lour Burn where it meets the River Spey. It stands at the Well of St. Drostan, who was one of St. Columba's disciples and went on to become Archbishop of Canterbury in 960AD. It was founded in 1879 by the philanthropist James Fleming, whose motto "Let The Deed Show" appears on every bottle. Following a fire in 1898, which started in the malt mill and destroyed most of the distillery was

rebuilt by the architect Charles Doig of Elgin. Further improvements were made in the 1920s, after World War II, in the 1960s, and in the 1970s.

Exceptionally soft water is drawn from springs in the Lour Glen, having flowed through peat, over the hard granite hills surrounding Ben Rinnes. The distillery is oil-fired, and uses a stainless steel mash tun, 4 stainless steel washbacks, and 4 pot stills. The malt is supplied to order and is lightly peated. Aberlour malt whiskies have benefited from greater use of oloroso sherry casks in recent years which, combined with bourbon casks, add to the whisky's complexity.

Aberlour 10 years old (profiled) has been awarded the International Wine and Spirit Competition's Gold Medal on several occasions. Aberlour malt whiskies are also available at 12 years old and 15 years old Sherry Wood finish,

Feature	Profile
●●●	Body
●●●	Sweetness
●	Smoky
	Medicinal
	Tobacco
●●●●	Honey
●●●	Spicy
●●	Winey
●●	Nutty
●●●	Malty
●●●	Fruity
●●	Floral

Age 10 years
Strength 40%
Nose Spicy, estery and sherried, showing pear-drops, pine and mint-toffee
Taste Medium-bodied, medium-sweet and multi-layered. Honey evident with nutmeg, autumn fruits and mint toffee notes, and a whiff of smoke in the finish
Cluster B Medium-bodied, medium-sweet, with nutty, malty, floral, honey and fruity notes
Similar to Strathisla, Benrinnes, Benromach

at 12 years old and 15 years old Double Cask Matured, at 30 years old, and special bottlings such as Aberlour 15 Year Old Cuvee Marie D'Ecosse, a cask-strength version not chill-filtered, and cask-strength Aberlour a'bunadh.

Aberlour distillery has a visitor centre offering an audio-visual presentation, tours and tastings from March to October. You can also visit www.aberlour.com and a newsletter is available by e-mail.

ALLT Á BHAINNE

{owlt-a'vanya}

Allt á Bhainne is Gaelic for "the milk burn", a spring where farmers would milk their cows in former times. It was built in 1975, and expanded in 1989, to supply malt whisky for Chivas Regal blends. Sitting prominently on the lower slopes of Benrinnes, near Dufftown, it has a sleek architectural design laid out internally all on one level for efficient operation.

The distillery draws its water from springs on Benrinnes, and uses un-peated barley malt. It operates a large stainless steel mash tun, 8 stainless steel washbacks and 4 stills. The lyne arms unusually incline upwards and the 2 spirit stills have boil balls in the necks. These features increase reflux, causing the heavier volatiles to fall back, and a lighter spirit results.

The mash tun is the only equipment that requires manual operation, everything else being computer-controlled, and hence the whole plant can be run by one man. Nevertheless the production capacity is high at 4 million litres of spirit a year. There are no warehouses at the distillery and the new spirit is transported by tanker for filling and maturation at Keith. It is mostly matured in ex-bourbon American oak refill casks, with a few sherry butts reserved for special malt editions.

Allt á Bhainne single malt has not been bottled by the producers, although a cask strength Chivas edition is in prospect, and it is therefore difficult to find. Signatory offer a nice decanter edition (pictured) at cask strength, non chill-filtered. It is also available in Gordon & MacPhail's Connoisseurs Choice range at 12 years old (profiled) from an ex-bourbon refill barrel, and from Cadenhead at 12 years old.

The distillery does not have a visitor centre or offer tours.

Feature	Profile
●	Body
●●●	Sweetness
●	Smoky
	Medicinal
●	Tobacco
●	Honey
●●	Spicy
	Winey
●	Nutty
●●	Malty
●●	Fruity
●●	Floral

Age 12 years
Strength 43%
Nose Light and floral, strawberries and cream, bubblegum and meadows
Taste Refreshing and sweet, with lemonade, custard, slightly spiced and toasted, aperitif style
Cluster E Light, medium-sweet, low peat, with floral, malty notes and fruity, spicy, honey hints
Similar to Glenallachie, Glenburgie, Glenlossie

AN CNOC

{*an*-CROCHK}

Knockdhu distillery was founded in 1894 by John Morrison, following the discovery of several springs of purest, crystal clear water on the southern slopes of Knock Hill. The location was perfect, being within a few miles of the fertile farmlands of Moray, a district noted for its barley, and on the edge of an inexhaustible supply of peat, essential ingredients in the making of an excellent malt whisky. The surrounding crofting community also offered an ideal source of labour, and for transport of supplies and whisky it was connected to the Great Highland railway line with its own station and siding.

The distillery is attractively constructed using local grey granite. Its malt mill was replaced in 1928, as the original exploded, on one occasion partly demolishing the still house, raising the roof and setting fire to the rafters.

During World War II Knockdhu housed a unit of the Indian Army, with stables and a slaughterhouse being constructed for the preparation of the soldiers' food.

After another closure, the distillery was reopened in 1989 and now produces excellent malt whiskies from its two original pot stills. During recent renovations, a message from John Smith of Huntly, who built the distillery in 1894, was found in a bottle under the plaster. It was replaced by a new time capsule, sealed in an empty bottle of An Cnoc, and buried in the stillhouse wall in 2001. The whisky is called "An Cnoc", which is Gaelic for "black hill" and is so named because of the natural spring water it draws from three springs on Knock Hill. It operates a traditional cast iron mash tun, 6 Oregon pine washbacks and 2 squat stills incorporating boil balls in the neck to increase reflux. The

profiled malt is An Cnoc 12 years old Single Highland Malt Scotch Whisky. There is a special edition An Cnoc vintage 1990, non chill-filtered, and a Knockdhu 23 years old cask strength edition.

An Cnoc does not have a visitor centre, but visitors are welcome by appointment.

Feature	Profile
●	Body
●●●	Sweetness
●●	Smoky
	Medicinal
	Tobacco
●●	Honey
	Spicy
	Winey
●●	Nutty
●●	Malty
●●●	Fruity
●●	Floral

Age 12 years
Strength 40%
Nose Lemon, honey and fruit aromas, with a hint of herbs
Taste Sweet and fairly complex with lots of fruit and nutty, creamy notes, and a whiff of smoke
Cluster D Light, medium-sweet, low or no peat, with fruity, floral, malty notes and nutty hints
Similar to Cardhu, Tamdhu, Aultmore

ARDBEG

{*ard*-BEG}

Ardbeg distillery was founded in 1815 by John MacDougall, on a site that had been a favourite landing spot for smugglers throughout the eighteenth century. It is in a remote, windswept cove on the south-east shore of Islay and is approached by a narrow road weaving through beautiful, rugged countryside. The sense of mystery and intrigue is heightened by the nearby Kildalton Cross, a sixth-century Celtic relic from Ardbeg's historic past.

Ardbeg's beautifully soft water flows from Loch Uigeadail through rocks and peat mosses to the distillery. It operates a stainless steel semi-Lauter mash tun, encased in the original cast iron tun, 6 Oregon pine washbacks and 2 large stills. An ancient "Boby mill" grinds the malted barley and the spirit still is fitted with a purifier before the condensers to partially cool the vapours and thus remove the heavier volatiles. The whisky is mostly matured in American oak ex-bourbon casks, with a few sherry butts reserved for special bottlings.

Ardbeg Single Islay Malt Scotch Whisky is available non chill-filtered at 10 years old (profiled). There is an annual release of Ardbeg from the first spirit distilled by the new owners in 1997. The range also includes Ardbeg Uigeadail, "Lord of the Isles" at 25 years old and special limited single cask editions.

A most atmospheric distillery, in which the old kiln and malt barn have been converted into a fine visitor centre, and where a friendly welcome awaits, it is a definite "must" for visitors to Islay. As well as touring the distillery and sampling the whiskies, you can enjoy lunch or afternoon tea in the Old Kiln Café, browse the shop and visit the gallery which tells the story of Ardbeg's past.

For those not able to visit Ardbeg in person, virtual tours are available at *ardbeg.com*. There is also an Ardbeg Committee whose members benefit from regular updates from the distillery and exclusive bottlings.

Feature	Profile
●●●●	Body
●	Sweetness
●●●●	Smoky
●●●●	Medicinal
	Tobacco
	Honey
●●	Spicy
	Winey
●	Nutty
●●	Malty
●	Fruity
	Floral

Age 10 years
Strength 46%
Nose Peaty, salty and malty with hints of bourbon and tangy orange
Taste Smoke and iodine evident with spice, cocoa and liquorice notes also showing
Cluster J Full-bodied, dry, pungent, peaty and medicinal, with spicy, tobacco notes
Similar to Talisker, Lagavulin, Caol Ila

ARDMORE

{*ard*-MORE}

rdmore distillery was built in 1898 by Adam Teacher for William Teacher & Sons. It is situated beside the River Bogie, in rolling countryside famed for its barley and Aberdeen Angus beef. Nearby is Leith Hall (see above), a picturesque seventeenth-century Scottish baronial mansion house with witches' hats for turrets and attractively themed gardens.

It is a large distillery, extended in 1955 and 1974, and is home to the principal malt of the Teacher's blends. The water is drawn from springs that rise in Knockandy Hill and its malted barley, supplied to order, is probably the most peated on Speyside. The distillery operates an interesting Boby mill, a fine copper-topped mash tun, 14 Oregon pine washbacks, 4 wash and 4 spirit pot stills. Three yeasts are used in the fermentation, which typically lasts 54 hours. The stills were converted from coal-fired to steam heating in 2001, increasing production capacity to around 70,000 litres (1.3 million pints) of spirit per week.

The whisky is matured at the distillery in American oak bourbon and refill casks. Most of Ardmore's production is used for blending in Teacher's Highland Cream. Ardmore 12 years old Single Highland Malt (profiled) was bottled in 1999 for the distillery's Centenary. It is difficult to find, as is a rather expensive 21 years old vintage. Other vintages are available from Gordon & MacPhail and Cadenhead.

Ardmore distillery has no visitor centre and does not offer tours. However, Ardmore single malts can be purchased at its sister distillery, Glendronach. Failing that, Teacher's Highland Cream is a blend that contains a high proportion of malt whiskies, with Ardmore well to the fore.

Feature	Profile
●●	Body
●●	Sweetness
●●	Smoky
	Medicinal
	Tobacco
●	Honey
●	Spicy
●	Winey
●●	Nutty
●●●	Malty
●	Fruity
●	Floral

Age 12 years
Strength 40%
Nose Medium sweet, creamy and smoky
Taste Mellow and malty, with balanced sweetness and buttery, oaky and peaty notes
Cluster F Medium-bodied, medium-sweet, low peat, malty notes and sherry, honey, spicy hints
Similar to Deanston, Fettercairn, Tomatin

ISLE OF ARRAN

{Arr-en}

I sle of Arran distillery was founded in 1995 at Lochranza village on the north of Arran, one of the most beautiful locations in Scotland. It is not uncommon to encounter deer beside the distillery or spot golden eagles circling the crags above Glen Chalmadale.

Arran has a long history of whisky-making. In the nineteenth century it is estimated that there were more than 50 whisky producers on Arran, most of which were illegal. It is not surprising, therefore, that the term "Arran Water" is synonymous with whisky, and at one time Arran whisky was said to be the best in Scotland. However, the island's remoteness and the cost of transportation forced the producers to close.

It took the inspirational leadership of the distillery's founder Harold Currie to resurrect the Arran whisky industry. The Isle of Arran distillery is of a modern, purpose-built design that cleverly incorporates a pagoda-chimney on the roof of its visitor centre and production buildings.

The distillery draws soft, peaty water from Loch na Davie and operates a stainless steel mash tun, 4 Oregon pine washbacks and 2 specially designed copper stills. The whisky is matured in a mixture of American white oak bourbon casks, and refill and fresh sherry European oak casks.

Isle of Arran single malt is available at 9 years old (profiled), and as non chill-filtered single cask editions from bourbon and sherry casks. Special finishes at cask strength include calvados, cognac, port, rum, marsala, Bordeaux and Champagne editions. The company also offers 3 blended whiskies – Glen Rosa, Lochranza and Robert Burns, and Arran Gold Cream Liqueur, which combines whisky with cream.

The visitor centre is open from March to October, and offers fully guided tours, an audio visual presentation set in a mock eighteenth century Crofter's Inn, an exhibition, shop and 5-star restaurant. The exhibition includes a smugglers' tunnel and a spectacular waterfall. It is highly commended by the Scottish Tourist Board, and in 2005 the company won the Queen's Award for Enterprise. It is definitely worth a visit when on Arran, and is a great place to stop for lunch.

Feature	Profile
●●	Body
●●●	Sweetness
●	Smoky
	Medicinal
	Tobacco
●	Honey
●	Spicy
●	Winey
●●	Nutty
●●	Malty
●●	Fruity
●●	Floral

Age 10 years
Strength 43%
Nose Aromatic and creamy, with oranges, lemons and cooking apples, and a hint of smoke
Taste Sweet and malty, with cream-toffee, honey, pistachios and citrus notes
Cluster D Light, medium-sweet, low or no peat with fruity, floral, malty notes and nutty hints
Similar to Cardhu, Speyside, Aultmore

AUCHENTOSHAN

{OCH-*en*-TOSH-*an*}

uchentoshan is Gaelic for "corner of the field". The distillery was first licensed in 1823 and is located in Dalmuir at the foot of the Kilpatrick hills. From its position on the Clyde, it has seen the evolution of shipping, from schooners such as the Cutty Sark to the Queen Elizabeth II on her maiden voyage. It was rebuilt in 1875, bombed in World War II, repaired in 1949, re-equipped in 1974, and refurbished in the late 1980s.

Auchentoshan is one of three distilleries classified as Lowland along with Bladnoch and Glenkinchie. It is the last Lowland distillery to employ triple distillation, whereby the output from the wash still is distilled twice more to produce a lighter, more

refined spirit. Its whisky has thereby earned the title of "The Lowland Malt".

The distillery's process water is supplied from Loch Katrine and its cooling water is collected in a World War II bomb crater in the hills. It uses unpeated malt, supplied to order, and operates a copper-topped stainless steel mash tun, 4 Oregon pine washbacks, and 3 stills. The spirit emerges from the wash still at 18% alcohol, at 54% from the intermediate still, and at 81% from the spirit still – the highest strength of any Scotch whisky. It is matured in a mixture of American bourbon and Spanish sherry casks, including some oloroso and sweet Pedro Ximénez sherry casks, specially prepared in Spain.

Auchentoshan Lowland Single Malt whisky is available at 10 years old (profiled), and as Auchentoshan Select, which has no age statement. Other bottlings are at 21, 22, 25 and 31 years old. There is also a "Three Wood" edition with no age statement, matured in American bourbon hogsheads, oloroso sherry and sweet Pedro Ximénez casks, and a cask strength 18 years old vintage 1978. The malts have won several international gold medals.

The distillery has a visitor centre that is open all year, for tours and tastings.

Feature	Profile
	Body
●●	Sweetness
	Smoky
	Medicinal
	Tobacco
●	Honey
●	Spicy
	Winey
●●	Nutty
●●	Malty
●●●	Fruity
●●●	Floral

Age 10 years
Strength 40%
Nose Fragrant, fresh and bursting with lemon zest
Taste Fruity citrus and raisins, muesli and satsumas, with a dusting of cinnamon
Cluster D Light, medium-sweet, low or no peat, with fruity, floral, malty notes and nutty hints
Similar to Glentauchers, Glengoyne, Cardhu

AUCHROISK

{otb-RUSK}

Auchroisk distillery was built in 1974 as a model distillery, with a showcase still-house containing eight lantern-headed pot stills arranged in two neat rows. Auchroisk is Gaelic for "ford across the red stream". It was felt that the name would be too difficult for customers to use so the malt it produces was called "The Singleton". A Victorian steam engine from Strathmill distillery is preserved as a showpiece in the entrance hall.

Auchroisk draws its water from Dorie's Well which is very soft, of exceptional quality, and the reason for the distillery's location. It operates a stainless steel mash tun, 8 stainless steel washbacks and 8 stills. The stills are high-necked with nearly horizontal lyne-arms, originally designed to produce a light, elegant spirit for use in J&B blends. Indeed, Auchroisk remains the heart of J&B, and the distillery carries out the vatting of the malt whisky constituents of those blends. The whisky is matured in American oak bourbon casks. However, it was among the first in the industry to apply a sherry finish to its malt whisky, which is finished in sherry casks for the final year.

Auchroisk Single Speyside Malt whisky (profiled) is available at 10 years old in Diageo's Flora and Fauna series. It was bottled as "The Singleton" at 10 years old, at 12 years old cask-strength, and in occasional vintage editions such as Auchroisk Rare Malt 28 years old distilled in 1974, the year of first production. It is also available through independent bottlers, but generally without any sherry wood finish. The Singleton was a highly regarded "designer" malt whisky that won several awards in international competitions. The emblem of

Feature	Profile
●●	Body
●●●	Sweetness
●	Smoky
	Medicinal
	Tobacco
●●	Honey
●	Spicy
●●	Winey
●●	Nutty
●●	Malty
●●	Fruity
●	Floral

Age 10 years
Strength 43%
Nose Fragrant and honeyed with a whiff of smoke
Taste Medium-bodied, apple crumble with sherry, nuts, autumn berries, and vanilla
Cluster F Medium-bodied, medium-sweet, low peat, malty notes and sherry, honey, spicy hints
Similar to Glenrothes, Deanston, Glen Keith

Auchroisk is the swift, which raise their young under the eaves of the distillery buildings.

Auchroisk distillery does not have a visitor centre or offer tours.

AULTMORE

{*olt*-MORE}

The Aultmore distillery was built by Alexander Edward Keith in 1895. Aultmore is Gaelic for "the big burn", which flows off the Foggie Moss. It was a favourite spot for illicit distilling in the early nineteenth century, due to the numerous springs in the hills and the plentiful supply of peat on the Foggie Moss. However, the distillery's location was chosen for its proximity to the Great North of Scotland Railway, to which it was connected by a siding from the Keith-Buckie line, and the village was built solely for the distillery workers. It suffered a major accident in the mid-1960s, when the brakes on the distillery train failed causing it to run amok, crashing into Keith station. Shortly afterwards the line was closed.

For almost three-quarters of a century the distillery was powered by a 10 horsepower Abernethy steam engine, with an elaborate system of line shafts and belts connecting all the moving processes. In its heyday, this was the last word in power efficiency and it is proudly retained as a feature in the entrance hall.

In the early 1950s, Aultmore distillery pioneered the production of "dark grains", or protein-rich animal feed, from the combination of the waste products of pot ale and draff. This process is now ubiquitous, and one of the reasons that the Scotch Whisky industry can justifiably claim to be ecologically efficient.

The distillery was completely rebuilt in 1971 with a doubled capacity and rather functional buildings. Water is drawn from the Auchinderran Burn, and the distillery operates a stainless steel Lauter mash tun, 6 Siberian larch washbacks and 4 stills. The mash tun is one of the most technically advanced in the industry, providing continuous sparging by which water is added continuously rather than in the more traditional batches. The arms move up and down while rotating and use a combination of rakes and blades to ensure maximum extraction of sugars.

Aultmore was sold with the Dewar's portfolio to Bacardi in 1998, hence its malt whisky was distilled by the previous

owners. The whisky is matured in American bourbon casks, refill hogsheads and sherry butts.

Aultmore Single Highland Malt whisky is available at 12 years old (profiled), and from independents. It is used in Dewar's blends, which currently account for the bulk of its production. The malt is difficult to find, but is stocked at Dewar's World of Whisky in Aberfeldy.

Aultmore distillery welcomes visitors by appointment.

Feature	Profile
●●	Body
●●	Sweetness
●	Smoky
	Medicinal
	Tobacco
●	Honey
	Spicy
	Winey
●●	Nutty
●●	Malty
●●	Fruity
●●	Floral

Age 12 years
Strength 40%
Nose Aromatic and fragrant, wet summer meadows
Taste Sweet and floral, grassy with hints of honey and spice
Cluster D Light, medium-sweet, low or no peat, with fruity, floral, malty notes and nutty hints
Similar to Speyside, Cardhu, Tobermory

BALBLAIR

{*bal*-BLAIR}

Founded in 1790 by John Ross, Balblair distillery is the industry's second oldest working distillery. It is situated in a beautiful part of the country, where the Allt Dearg Burns flow down the Struie Hill to the farmlands of Edderton (known as the "parish of the peats") on the shore of the Dornoch Firth. The distillery was rebuilt on a new site in 1894 and extended to 3 steam-heated stills in the 1960s. Its original riveted wash still is the only one of its type left in the industry. All its warehouses are earth-floored, except one that was converted by the army in World War II for use as a canteen.

The air in Edderton on the Dornoch Firth, where Balblair is distilled, is considered to be the purest in Scotland.

It has been swept across the vast expanse of the North Sea by Arctic winds, giving it a sharp clean edge; it has swirled around Cambuscurrie Bay, picking up a hint of saltiness; and has rushed through bristling coastal pine woods which imbue it with freshness. It is this pure air that is said to give Balblair whisky its smooth, light, delicate and refreshing taste.

In addition to the featured 10 years old Balblair Single Highland Malt Scotch Whisky, there is an un-aged version Balblair Elements, a 16 years old, and a 31 years old cask strength edition in the Highland Selection range. Balblair 16 years old Single Malt was awarded a Gold medal at the San Francisco World Spirits Competition in 2005.

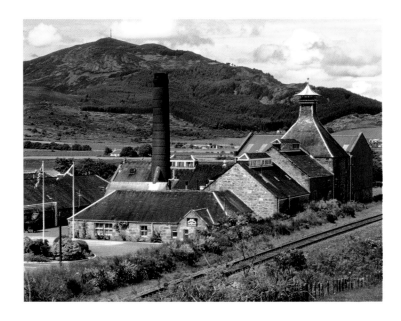

Balblair is one of the most attractive small distilleries and has remained largely unchanged since the nineteenth century. There is no visitor centre, but visitors are welcome by appointment.

Feature	Profile
●●	Body
●●●	Sweetness
●●	Smoky
●	Medicinal
	Tobacco
	Honey
●●	Spicy
	Winey
●●	Nutty
●	Malty
●●	Fruity
●	Floral

Age 10 years
Strength 40%
Nose Fresh with a smoky note and a touch of the sea
Taste Medium-sweet, with citrus fruits, and spicy, nutty and smoky notes
Cluster H Medium-bodied, medium-sweet, with smoky, fruity, spicy notes and floral, nutty hints
Similar to Craigellachie, Oban, Glenmorangie

BALMENACH

{*bal*-MEN-*ach*}

Ballindalloch Castle in the Hills of Cromdale.

Established by smugglers who came over the hills from Tomintoul, Balmenach distillery was one of the earliest to be licensed by James McGregor in 1824, at a time when illicit distilling was a way of life. Situated above the village of Cromdale, one of the crossing points of the River Spey, the distillery stands on historic soil. On the nearby hill of Tom Lethendry are the ruins of an old castle where, in 1690, the defeated Jacobites took refuge after the battle of the Haughs of Cromdale. The distillery was reconstructed in 1920, extended to 6 stills in 1962 and had its mash-house rebuilt in 1968. After a period of inactivity, it was acquired by Inver House Distillers in 1997 and has been restored to full working order.

Its water is drawn from Rasmudin Burn, and the distillery operates a traditional copper-domed cast iron mash tun, 6 Oregon pine washbacks and 6 squat stills incorporating boil balls in their necks to increase reflux. One wash still has a decorative collar commemorating its use in Hyde Park during Queen Elizabeth's Silver Jubilee celebrations in 1977. It still uses worm tub condensers, which allow longer contact with copper for extended catalysis, and indeed everything about Balmenach is "old fashioned". The whisky is matured in a mixture of American bourbon, European sherry and refill casks, in traditional dunnage warehouses. Balmenach Single Highland Malt whisky is only available in special editions, such as 27 years old "Highland Selection" (46%), and through independents. We look forward to the new, less peated whisky in about 2009. The distillery has no visitor centre, but visitors are very welcome.

Feature	Profile
●●●●	Body
●●●	Sweetness
●●	Smoky
	Medicinal
	Tobacco
●●	Honey
●	Spicy
●●●	Winey
●●●	Nutty
	Malty
●	Fruity
●●	Floral

Age 12 years
Strength 43%
Nose Aromatic, floral and nutty with a sherried nose and a whiff of smoke
Taste Full bodied, medium sweet, with vanilla, honey and sherry notes, and a spicy finish
Cluster A Full-bodied, medium-sweet, pronounced sherry with fruity, spicy, malty notes and nutty, smoky hints
Similar to Mortlach, Dailuaine, Macallan

BALVENIE

{bal-VENN-ee}

Balvenie distillery takes its name from Balvenie Castle, where it was founded in 1892 by William Grant, who also built Glenfiddich distillery next door. Some of the barley used by the distillery is grown on its own farm, and it is one of the few to have retained traditional floor maltings, where the germinating grain is turned by hand three times a day using traditional wooden shiels.

It is an attractive Victorian distillery whose buildings have remained largely unchanged for a century. The maltings boast a single pagoda vent, and the kilns are still fired by coal and peat. The distillery operates a stainless steel mash tun, 10 Douglas fir washbacks, 4 wash stills and 5 spirit stills. Its water is drawn from springs on the Conval Hills, and the whisky is matured using a larger proportion of European sherry casks than Glenfiddich. The distillery normally uses lightly peated malt, but it has also been producing some whisky from heavily peated malt since 2002. Balvenie also has its own coopers to maintain the casks, and a coppersmith to tend the stills.

Balvenie distillery produces Founder's Reserve 10 years old (profiled), Balvenie DoubleWood 12 years old, Balvenie PortWood 1991, and Balvenie Single Barrel at 15 and 30 years old. DoubleWood is first matured in a traditional American bourbon cask and then finished in an original sherry oak cask; PortWood is similarly finished in port pipes, adding a pink hue and a rich fruity taste. This special cask finishing modifies the flavour of DoubleWood and PortWood to the style of cluster A. Their rare malts include Balvenie PortWood 21 years old, Balvenie Vintage Cask 1973, and Balvenie Cask 191 at 50 years old.

A new visitor centre opened in 2005 offering tours and tastings, including the cooperage and floor maltings during the malting season – advance booking is advised. Internet visitors to *thebalvenie.com* can join the Balvenie Club to receive news and special offers.

Feature	Profile
●●●	Body
●●	Sweetness
●	Smoky
	Medicinal
	Tobacco
●●●	Honey
●●	Spicy
●	Winey
	Nutty
●●	Malty
●●	Fruity
●●	Floral

Age 10 years
Strength 40%
Nose Rich and complex. with honey and orange notes and a hint of smoke
Taste Medium-bodied honey sweet, with light spicy notes and a hint of sherry fruitiness. The finish is long and rich
Cluster C Medium-bodied, medium-sweet, with fruity, floral, honey, malty notes and spicy hints
Similar to Benriach, Glen Ord, Glendullan

BEN NEVIS

{*ben*-NEV-*is*}

Ben Nevis distillery was built in 1825 by John Macdonald, a farmer from Wester Ross, and his whisky was sold as "Long John's Dew of Ben Nevis". The name stuck and was later used for a blend called "Long John", which is sadly no longer available. Queen Victoria visited the distillery during her tour of Scotland in 1848, and the distillery subsequently sent a barrel of whisky to Buckingham Palace for the Prince of Wales's 21st birthday.

The distillery was rebuilt in 1865, and there were further modifications in 1887, when a pier was added on Loch Linnhe, and in 1894 when it was connected to the West Highland Railway. A Coffey still was introduced in 1955 to produce grain whisky, thereby enabling Ben Nevis distillery to make blended whisky.

Its water is drawn from Allt a Mhullin "the Mill Stream" which flows from two small lochs on the north face of Ben Nevis, Britain's highest mountain. The distillery operates a large stainless steel mash tun, 6 stainless steel washbacks and 4 swan-necked pot stills – producing some 750,000 litres (1.3 million pints) a year. The whisky is matured in 7 warehouses at the distillery, using ex-bourbon American oak and ex-sherry European oak casks.

Ben Nevis Single Highland Malt whisky is available at 10 years old (profiled). It is also used in the Ben Nevis Special Reserve blend, and in a dew of Ben Nevis 12 years old *de luxe* blend. The 10 years old malt won Grand Gold Medals at the Mondé Selection de la Qualité, Belgium in 1999 and 2000, Gold Medals in 2001 and 2003 and a trophy in 2001.

The distillery's visitor centre in a former warehouse dating from 1862, offers tours, tastings, a "Legend of the Dew of Ben Nevis" audio-visual presentation, an exhibition, a coffee shop and restaurant.

Feature	Profile
●●●●	Body
●●	Sweetness
●●	Smoky
	Medicinal
	Tobacco
●●	Honey
●●	Spicy
	Winey
●●	Nutty
●●	Malty
●●	Fruity
●●	Floral

Age 10 years
Strength 46%
Nose Aromatic and estery, with some spice and smoke evident
Taste Creamy caramels, fruit and oak, with a peaty finish – a very well-balanced profile
Cluster B Medium-bodied, medium-sweet, with nutty, malty, floral, honey and fruity notes
Similar to Benromach, Benrinnes

BENRIACH

{ben-REE-ach}

BenRiach is Gaelic for the "hill of the red deer", and wild red stags can sometimes be heard roaring in the Teindland Forest nearby. The distillery is named after Riach Farm, where it was built in 1898 by John Duff, who also built Longmorn distillery next door. The location was chosen for the quality of its water and its proximity to the Great North of Scotland Railway, to which it was connected by a siding from Longmorn Station (pictured).

However, the distillery closed in 1900 after just two years of production, following the Pattison Crash and the downturn in the whisky industry. It remained silent until 1965, except for its floor maltings, which continued in use throughout this period to supply Longmorn distillery next door. It ceased production again in 2002, but restarted in 2004 under its new private owners, a dynamic team that promises to bring a great new future for BenRiach.

It is a delightful, Victorian stone distillery with a pagoda chimney which is a landmark in the Glen of Rothes. The water source is Burnside Spring which rises through rock below the distillery, and it uses both un-peated and peated malted barley for separate runs. It operates a stainless steel mash tun, 8 stainless steel washbacks, 2 medium-sized wash stills and 2 medium-sized spirit stills. The whisky is matured in a mixture of American bourbon barrels, European sherry casks, and refills. Current production is 1.5 million litres of alcohol per year, about 70% of full capacity. The present whiskies were produced before the distillery converted to steam heating, using barley malted at the distillery on traditional floor maltings that continued in use until 1999. The kiln, with its distinctive pagoda chimney, was sometimes fired with peat cut from Mannoch Hill to produce peated, malted barley and this enables BenRiach to capture the original flavour of "peat reek" in a few special bottlings. Some of the whisky goes for blending, but significant stocks are laid down for future use as single malts.

BenRiach Single Highland Malt is available at 12 years old (profiled) at 16 and 20 years old, and in special editions such as 1986, 1974 and 1966

vintages. It is also available as BenRiach "Curiositas" 10 years old and BenRiach "Authenticus" 21 years old, both of which are distinctly smoky, and as an unaged BenRiach "Heart of Speyside" single malt. Current editions can be found at *benriachdistillery.co.uk.*

BenRiach distillery has plans for a visitor centre and tours can be arranged by appointment.

Feature	Profile
●●	Body
●●	Sweetness
●	Smoky
	Medicinal
	Tobacco
●●	Honey
●●	Spicy
	Winey
	Nutty
●●	Malty
●●●	Fruity
●●	Floral

Age 12 years
Strength 43%
Nose Light and fruity with a honey sweetness
Taste Medium bodied, summer fruits with caramel and cumin seed, and a hint of smoke
Cluster C Medium-bodied, medium-sweet, with fruity, floral, honey, malty notes and spicy hints
Similar to Dalwhinnie, Balvenie, Glen Ord

BENRINNES

{ben-RIN-is}

Lying high on Ben Rinnes, whose 840-metre (2,800-feet) summit dominates Speyside and the Moray Firth, is the rather remote and functional Benrinnes distillery. Because of its height, supplies were originally brought by horse and cart from Aberlour station, three miles away. The emblem on the bottle is the blackcock, a resident of the surrounding moors.

In 1826, Peter McKenzie of Whitehouse Farm was recorded as the licensed distiller. The distillery moved to its present site in 1829 following a flood, and by 1842 it existed as a farm whose outbuildings were used for distillation. Benrinnes was still a working farm a century later, with distillery traffic being frequently delayed by the twice-daily procession of cattle for milking. Occasionally the cows took fright, at which the distillery workers would down tools and round them up. The farming element was removed in the mid-1950s when the Benrinnes distillery was rebuilt and, in 1966, a

Saladin malting was added and the still house was extended to 6 stills. Today malted barley is supplied to order, lightly peated. Water is drawn from springs that rise on Ben Rinnes, passing over granite, through peat and moss, and finally being filtered on the gravel beds of the Rowantree and Scurran burns.

The distillery operates a stainless steel mash tun, 8 Oregon pine washbacks, 2 wash stills and 4 spirit stills. The stills are grouped in threes because some of the spirit is triple-distilled, the output from each wash still being split between an intermediate and a spirit still. The intermediate still is used to re-distill the feints or weak low wines produced by all three stills. Another unusual feature is the use of traditional worm tubs to condense the spirit, rather than the more modern condenser method. Although triple distillation would normally yield a lighter style of whisky, the smaller intermediate spirit still and worm-tub condensers afford greater contact with

copper for extended catalysis, resulting in a full flavoured whisky.

The whisky is matured in a combination of bourbon and sherry casks. Most goes for blending, though the 15 years old Benrinnes Single Malt (profiled) is available in Diageo's Flora and Fauna range, in their Rare Malts series at 21 years old (60.4%), and in Gordon & MacPhail's Connoisseurs Choice range.

The distillery does not have a visitor centre or offer tours.

Feature	Profile
●●●	Body
●●	Sweetness
●●	Smoky
	Medicinal
	Tobacco
●●●	Honey
●	Spicy
●	Winey
●●	Nutty
●●●	Malty
●●	Fruity
●●	Floral

Age 15 years
Strength 43%
Nose Soft, medium-dry, with a little peat and cereal
Taste Medium-sweet, smooth, slightly smoky with grassy, flowery notes
Cluster B Medium-bodied, medium-sweet, with nutty, malty, floral, honey and fruity notes
Similar to Benromach, Aberfeldy, Ben Nevis

SPEYSIDE
SINGLE MALT
SCOTCH WHISKY

BENRINNES

distillery stands on the *northern shoulder of BEN RINNES* 700 feet above *sea level*. It is ideally located to exploit the *natural advantages* of the area-pure *air*, *peat* and *barley* and the *finest* of *hill* water, which rises through *granite* from *springs* on the *summit* of the *mountain*. The resulting *single MALT SCOTCH WHISKY*, is *rounded* and *mellow*.

AGED **15** YEARS

Distilled & Bottled in SCOTLAND
BENRINNES DISTILLERY
Aberlour, Banffshire, Scotland.

43% vol 70 cl

BENROMACH

{*ben*-ROM-*ach*}

Benromach distillery was designed in 1898 by Charles Doig, the noted Elgin architect who was responsible for several other Speyside distilleries. Its original buildings were modernised in 1966, and extended in 1974 and 1998. The distillery has had a chequered career, with several changes of ownership and dormant periods, the last closure being in 1983 when all the distillation equipment was removed. Happily, it was rescued in 1993 by Gordon & MacPhail, the Elgin whisky merchants, and production re-commenced in 1998. Benromach's whitewashed buildings and tall red brick chimney create a striking local landmark in the lush arable landscape of the Laich of Moray on the northern edge of Forres.

Process water is drawn from the Romach Hills and *Chariot* barley is supplied lightly peated to order. Benromach operates a large stainless steel mash tun, 4 larch washbacks and 2 traditional steam-heated stills. The stills are shorter than most to distil a full, rich spirit, and are currently producing about 0.5 million litres a year. The malt whiskies are matured in traditional dunnage warehouses using new Spanish sherry casks, while the whisky for use in blends is matured in American oak bourbon barrels and refill sherry casks.

Benromach Traditional Speyside Malt whisky (profiled) was the first to be produced by the new distillery, and contrasts with the whiskies distilled under the previous management, which are available as Benromach 21 years old, 25 years old and cask strength. Special finishes include Benromach Port Wood, and the unusual Benromach Tokaji 21 years old finished in casks seasoned with the sweet Hungarian wine, Tokaji. There are also special vintages including Benromach 1968 and Benromach Classic 55 years old. Benromach malt whiskies have won several awards in international competitions.

A former drier house was converted in 1999 to a Malt Whisky Centre and shop, which has been graded as a 4-star attraction by the Scottish Tourist Board. It includes a fine "Heritage Room"

where the story of malt whisky is told. Benromach distillery offers tours and tastings all year. Visitors also have the opportunity to bottle their own personal Benromach edition straight from the cask.

Feature	Profile
●●	Body
●●	Sweetness
●●	Smoky
	Medicinal
	Tobacco
●●	Honey
●●	Spicy
●	Winey
●●	Nutty
●●	Malty
●●	Fruity
●●	Floral

Age 5 years
Strength 40%
Nose Aromatic and floral, with a hint of sherry
Taste Fruity, herbal and malty notes with hints of spice
Cluster B Medium-bodied, medium-sweet, with nutty, malty, floral, honey and fruity notes
Similar to Blair Athol, Aberfeldy, Scapa

BLADNOCH

{BLAD-*noch*}

B ladnoch distillery was built in 1817 beside the River Bladnoch, by Thomas McClelland, and was rebuilt in 1871 by his grandson. It was extended in 1966, but suffered periods of closure, most recently in 1993. Happily, it was bought in 2000 by Ulsterman Raymond Armstrong, and is now once again in production, though limited to a fraction of its former capacity by a covenant imposed by the previous owners. The distinctive pagoda chimney, which reaches above the rest of the riverside complex, was once used to malt the barley grown by the McClellands, who originally started the distillery in the nineteenth century. It is one of only three working distilleries classified as Lowland, the others being Auchentoshan and Glenkinchie.

Along the riverside walk above the distillery is the ancient oak woodland of Cotland Wood; and in the pastures nearby can be seen a regional breed of black-faced sheep, the Belted Galloway, which is the emblem on the bottle. It will be some years before the spirit currently being produced is available to buy, but in the meantime there are existing stocks from the previous owners, prior to the closure in 1993.

Water is drawn from the River Bladnoch and the distillery operates a stainless steel mash tun, 6 Oregon pine washbacks and 2 tall pot stills, which incorporate boil balls in the neck. These boil balls help to cool the vapours so that the heavier volatiles fall back as reflux, resulting in a lighter spirit. The whisky is matured in a mixture of ex-bourbon American oak and ex-sherry European oak casks in the warehouses on the site.

Bladnoch Single Lowland Malt Whisky is available at different ages,

hand-bottled at the distillery. These include Bladnoch 16 years old (profiled), cask strength whisky that is not chill-filtered, and other editions depending on the availability of stock.

The visitor centre is open all year, and offers tours, tastings and a shop. There is also a residential Whisky School, where students work with the distillery team and learn whisky distillation skills.

Feature	Profile
●	Body
●●	Sweetness
●	Smoky
	Medicinal
	Tobacco
	Honey
●	Spicy
●	Winey
	Nutty
●●	Malty
●●	Fruity
●●●	Floral

Age 16 years
Strength 43%
Nose Aromatic and fruity, packed with flowers and citrus fruits
Taste Moderately sweet and fruity, with a cereal note, and hints of sherry and smoke
Cluster E Light, medium-sweet, low peat, with floral, malty notes and fruity, spicy, honey hints
Similar to Bunnahabhain, Glenburgie, Caperdonich

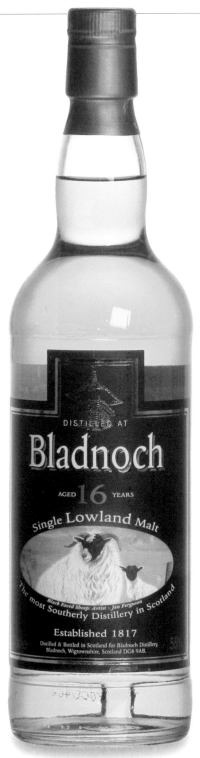

BLAIR ATHOL

{blair-ATH-oll}

The attractive, ivy-clad visitor centre at Blair Athol distillery (left), and the shop and bar (right).

The Blair Athol distillery was originally founded in 1798 by John Stewart and Robert Robertson, and was called "Aldour" after Allt Dour meaning "the burn of the otter". It lies on the edge of Pitlochry, in the Vale of Athol, which has long been famous for its whisky. Legend has it that the "mellow barley bree from the cavern of Ben-y-Vrackie warmed the hearts and strengthened the arms of the Highlanders" when they defeated the army of William III at Killiecrankie in 1689.

The distillery operates an 8 tonne stainless steel Lauter mash tun, 4 stainless steel washbacks, 4 Oregon pine washbacks and 4 copper stills. The barley is supplied un-peated to order, from Glen Ord maltings. Process water is drawn from the Allt Dour, which flows from a spring high on Ben-y-Vrackie and otters, one of which features on the distillery's bottles, can occasionally be sighted in the burn. Blair Athol's malt whiskies are matured in a mixture of ex-bourbon American refill casks and European oak sherry butts.

Blair Athol Single Malt is available at 12 years old (profiled) in Diageo's Flora and Fauna range, and also in the Rare Malts range at 27 years old. It is the heart of Bell's blends, which take more than 95% of its production.

The visitor centre is very popular due to its proximity to Edinburgh and Glasgow, and is open all year. It offers tours, tastings and a shop.

Feature	Profile
●●	Body
●●	Sweetness
●●	Smoky
	Medicinal
	Tobacco
●	Honey
●●	Spicy
●●	Winey
●●	Nutty
●●	Malty
●●	Fruity
●●	Floral

Age 12 years
Strength 43%
Nose Light and dry, aromatic with honey and citrus notes
Taste Strong fruity flavour, hints of sweetness and spice with a smoky finish
Cluster B Medium-bodied, medium-sweet, with nutty, malty, floral, honey and fruity notes
Similar to Aberfeldy, Benromach, Glenturret

HIGHLAND
SINGLE MALT
SCOTCH WHISKY

BLAIR ATHOL

distillery, established in 1798, stands on *peaty moorland* in the *foothills* of the *GRAMPIAN MOUNTAINS*. An ancient source of *water* for the *distillery, ALLT DOUR BURN ~ 'The Burn of the Otter',* flows close by. This *single MALT SCOTCH WHISKY* has a *mellow deep toned* aroma, a *strong fruity* flavour and a *smooth* finish.

12

45% vol   70 cl

Distilled & Bottled in SCOTLAND
BLAIR ATHOL DISTILLERY, Pitlochry, Perthshire, Scotland

BOWMORE

{*bow*-MORE}

With its classic whitewashed buildings and black trimmed windows, Bowmore distillery settles expansively along the shore of Loch Indaal, its pagoda-topped chimneys rising grandly above the town's high street. While its frontage is unmistakably Islay, with one seashore warehouse emblazoned "BOWMORE" in large bold letters, its malts have a fine character all their own.

It is the oldest licensed distillery on Islay, founded in 1779 by farmer David Simpson, and one of the first to offer its product widely as a single malt whisky. In the 1880s and 1890s, Bowmore Islay whisky was sold throughout Britain, Ireland and Canada. The focal point of the town is a round church at the top of the hill, with no corners in which the devil could hide. This is certainly a distillery rich in legends – indeed, its most popular single malt is named Bowmore Legend.

The management flirted briefly with stainless steel washbacks in the 1980s, but reverted to traditional wooden washbacks and floor maltings in the 1990s. Half its barley is still malted by hand on a traditional malting floor and dried over a peat fire, the peat being first crumbled to generate more smoke. Bowmore is only medium peated, however, with about half the phenols of its neighbours round the coast at Lagavulin, Laphroaig and Ardbeg, and as such it is not typically Islay.

Its water is drawn from the river Laggan and it operates a copper-domed mash tun, 6 Oregon pine washbacks and 4 pot stills. The whisky is matured in Spanish and American oak casks, some stored in the famous Bowmore Vaults below sea level, and about a third are prepared with oloroso sherry. Bowmore's award-winning heat recovery system uses the warm water from the condensers to pre-heat the mashing water, wash, and low wines.

Bowmore Single Islay Malt whisky is available at 12 years old (profiled), and at 15, 17, 21, 25, 30 and 40 years old. It is also offered as Bowmore Legend, a cask strength version with no age statement, and Darkest Islay, finished in oloroso sherry casks. Other expressions are named Dawn, Dusk, Surf, Mariner and Claret, Bowmore Cask Strength and there are also cask strength vintages such as a 1974 oloroso cask and a 1989 bourbon cask, non chill-filtered.

Bowmore distillery has an excellent visitor centre offering an audio-visual presentation, tours and tastings. The visitor centre and a well-stocked shop are open all year.

Feature	Profile
●●	Body
●●	Sweetness
●●●	Smoky
●●	Medicinal
	Tobacco
●●	Honey
●●	Spicy
●	Winey
●	Nutty
●	Malty
●	Fruity
●●	Floral

Age 12 years
Strength 40%
Nose Grassy and smoky, with a lemon note, and hints of sherry and seaweed
Taste Well balanced complexity with smoke, spice, heather, honey and chocolate
Cluster I Medium-light, dry, with smoky, spicy, honey notes and nutty, floral hints
Similar to Highland Park, Springbank, Bruichladdich

BOWMORE
ISLAY
Single Malt
SCOTCH WHISKY
Aged 12 Years
DISTILLED AND BOTTLED IN SCOTLAND
700 ml e   MORRISON'S BOWMORE DISTILLERY
ISLAY SCOTLAND   40% Vol.

BRAEVAL

{*bray*-VAL}

Braeval distillery is located high in the isolated Braes of Glenlivet, in the hamlet of Chapeltown, close to an ancient whisky trail. In the period 1780–1830, numerous small illicit whisky stills were hidden in the secluded hills, and the whisky they produced was smuggled south and east across the Ladder hills.

The distillery looks like a church, but sits incongruously beside the actual Victorian Church of Our Lady of Perpetual Succour. It was built in 1972 to meet the needs of the Seagram group for single malt components of Chivas Regal blends. Initially known as Braes of Glenlivet, its name was changed to Braeval in 1995 to avoid confusion with Glenlivet further down the glen.

The distillery has a fine pagoda roof despite having no maltings. Its architecture was modelled on a traditional distillery design, but internally the modern plant can be operated by one man with computer controls.

The water source is Preenie Well, fed by springs on Benrinnes, and it uses un-peated, malted barley. It operates a copper-domed stainless steel mash tun, 15 stainless steel washbacks and 6 stills, of which 2 are wash stills and 4 spirit. This combination is not designed for triple distillation, but rather each batch of low wines is used to charge 2 small spirit stills fitted with boil balls in the necks. The use of small stills, with long lyne arms inclined upwards, maintains a higher contact with copper which increases catalysis and a lighter, more estery spirit results.

The new spirit is reduced using spring water in large stainless steel receivers, then taken by tanker for filling and maturation in Keith. Most of the whisky is matured in American ex-bourbon casks, although a few special casks have been bottled by Signatory and Cadenhead.

Braeval Single Speyside Malt whisky is available in Gordon & MacPhail's Connoisseurs range 1975 vintage (profiled) and by Deerstalker at 10 years old, non chill-filtered. Bottled as Braes of Glenlivet, it is also available from Cadenheads at 8 and 10 years old.

The distillery does not have a visitor centre or offer tours.

Feature	Profile
●	Body
●●	Sweetness
●	Smoky
	Medicinal
	Tobacco
●	Honey
●●●	Spicy
	Winey
●	Nutty
●	Malty
●●	Fruity
●●●	Floral

Age 12 years
Strength 43%
Nose Light and dry, aromatic with honey and citrus notes
Taste Strong fruity flavour, hints of sweetness and spice with a smoky finish
Cluster B Medium-bodied, medium-sweet, with nutty, malty, floral, honey and fruity notes
Similar to Aberfeldy, Benromach, Glenturret

BOTTLED 2005

CONNOISSEURS CHOICE

SPEYSIDE
Single Malt Scotch Whisky

DISTILLED AT
BRAES OF GLENLIVET
DISTILLERY
Proprietors: Chivas Bros. Ltd.

DISTILLED
1975

Specially selected, produced and bottled by
Gordon & MacPhail
Elgin Scotland
Product of Scotland

70cl   43% vol

BRUICHLADDICH

{*brook*-LADDIE}

Bruichladdich distillery was purpose-built in 1881 by Barnet Harvey. In 1887, Alfred Barnard described it as "a solid handsome structure in the form of a square, entered through an archway over which is a fine stone-built residence". If he were to return today, he would not be disappointed, for little has changed. Its orderly, whitewashed buildings are etched with dark blue and aquamarine windows and, on entering the inner courtyard through the cast iron arch, you will discover that it has a unique charm of its own. It has had several silent periods, most recently in the late 1990s. Happily, it was bought privately in 2000 and is working again with a new, inspired team. Except for the kiln, demolished by a previous owner, all its Victorian equipment has been restored and is run in the traditional way – the team boasts "C'est dans les vieilles marmites qu'on fait la meilleure cuisine".

The soft spring water filters through hard quartz and softer sandstone of the Rhinns of Islay, emerging cold and crystal clear at the Octomore spring. The distillery operates an original nineteenth-century cast iron mash tun, 6 Oregon pine washbacks and 4 swan-necked stills. In addition to the lightly peated Bruichladdich, the distillery also produces medium-peated Port Charlotte, heavily peated Octomore, and triple distilled Trestarig, some of which can be reserved by the cask. The whisky is matured in ex-bourbon and sherry refill casks, in warehouses beside Loch Indaal. It is bottled at the distillery, reduced by water from the Octomore Spring, without any colouring, chill-filtration or homogenisation, hence it is truly a "château-bottled" malt.

Bruichladdich Single Islay Malt whisky, known familiarly as "the Laddie", is available at 10 years old (profiled), and at 15, 17, 20 and 40 years old. There are special editions such as Bruichladdich Celtic Heartlands; Centenary, Flirtation, Full Strength, Infinity, Legacy, Links, Mission, and 3D. Vintages are also available – for example a rare 1973

bourbon cask. It's impossible to keep up with this flamboyant, energetic team.

The distillery welcomes visitors and offers tours, tastings and special events. Fill your own bottle from the cask using a valinch, a glass pipette traditionally used to draw samples. Join the Bruichladdich whisky academy and discover the secrets of whisky-making while working with the distillery team. Plan ahead, and meet 1500 other devotees at their Open Day in May. If you cannot get to Islay, check out their live web-cams at *bruichladdich.com*.

Feature	Profile
●	Body
●	Sweetness
●●	Smoky
●●	Medicinal
	Tobacco
●●	Honey
●●	Spicy
●	Winey
●●	Nutty
●●	Malty
●●	Fruity
●●	Floral

Age 10 years
Strength 46%
Nose Fragrant, fruity and youthful, honeysuckle, summer fruits, a salty tang and whiff of smoke
Taste Light, medium dry with subtle complexity of honey, citrus fruits, toasted malt and almonds. Exceptionally well balanced
Cluster I Medium-light, dry, with smoky, spicy, honey notes and nutty, floral hints
Similar to Bowmore, Isle of Jura, Springbank

BUNNAHABHAIN

{BUNNA-*hah-ven*}

Westering home with a song in the air
Light in the eye and it's goodbye to care
Laughter o'love and a welcoming there
Isle of my heart my own one.

Bunnahabhain is Gaelic for "mouth of the river". The distillery was built by William and James Greenlees in 1881 at the confluence of the River Margadale with the Sound of Islay. The site was chosen for its abundant supplies of peat and clear water, and its accessibility to the sea. The buildings are of local stone and it was once a traditional distillery community with workers' cottages and a schoolhouse.

This is one of the few distilleries that offers accommodation. Visitors can rent one of the cottages, soak up the atmosphere and enjoy the spectacular views across to the Paps of Jura. The label on the bottle depicts a mariner at the helm of his ship, happily sighting Bunnahabhain as he threads through the Sound of Islay on his way home to Oban or Glasgow, and singing the traditional Scottish ballad "Westering Home".

Bunnahabhain is an excellent example of why the traditional method of regional classification no longer applies. Its whisky used to be heavily peated when local peat fuelled the kilns, and it was therefore typically Islay. However, early in the twentieth century Bunnahabhain departed from this tradition, and its principal spirit is made from lightly peated malted barley. Since the distillery changed hands in 2003, it has been producing a heavily peated Moinè spirit, which will become available from 2006.

The process water is collected in a reservoir from Margadale Springs and piped to the distillery. Bunnahabhain operates a stainless steel mash tun, 6 Oregon pine washbacks, and 4 large stills – the wash stills are onion-shaped whereas the spirit stills are smaller and more pear-shaped. The whisky is matured in ex-bourbon American oak barrels, and a small proportion of ex-sherry European oak casks.

Bunnahabhain Single Islay Malt whisky is available at 12 years old (profiled), at 18 and 25 years old, and in special Islay Whisky Festival editions. The 2005 Festival cask-strength edition was finished in port pipes and is bottled by hand at the distillery. It is the heart and home of the Black Bottle blend, and is also used in Scottish Leader, Cutty Sark and Famous Grouse blends.

Tours and tastings are available during summer.

Feature	Profile
●	Body
●●	Sweetness
●	Smoky
●	Medicinal
	Tobacco
●	Honey
●	Spicy
●	Winey
●	Nutty
●●	Malty
●●	Fruity
●●●	Floral

Age 12 years
Strength 40%
Nose Aromatic and fresh, with a whiff of smoke
Taste Light, fruity and malty, with hints of honey, walnuts and spice
Cluster E Light, medium-sweet, low peat, with floral, malty notes and fruity, spicy, honey hints
Similar to Glenburgie, Loch Lomond, Caperdonich

CAOL ILA

*{kowel-*EEL-*ah}*

Caol Ila is Gaelic for the "Sound of Islay", the strait that separates the islands of Islay and Jura. The distillery was founded by Hector Henderson in 1846, in a remote cove near Port Askaig on the Isle of Islay. It was extended in 1879 and completely modernised in 1972–74. Until 1972, the *Pibroch*, a small working steamship owned by the company, delivered barley, empty casks and coal to Caol Ila's pier, returning to Glasgow with casks filled with whisky. Today, everything is despatched by road and ferry to the mainland.

In 1886 Alfred Barnard described its location as the wildest and most picturesque he had seen, observing that "Comfortable dwellings have been provided for the employees, forming quite a little village in themselves, and we envied the healthy life of these men and their families." There was even a Mission Hall, where services were held every Sunday for the local community. Sadly, the original stone buildings and pagoda vents have been replaced by a functional modern distillery. Yet Caol Ila still remains atmospheric, particularly on a clear winter's night when the lights from the magnificent glass-fronted stillroom (pictured) can be seen right across the sound to Jura.

The distillery draws its process water from Loch nam Ban (Torrabolls Loch). Malted barley is supplied to order from Port Ellen Maltings, with various levels of peating. It operates a copper-domed stainless steel mashtun, 8 Canadian pine washbacks and 6 large stills. An unusual sea-water condenser cools the water from

the stills, which is then recycled owing to the scarcity of cooling water in summer.

Caol Ila whisky is used principally for the Johnnie Walker and Bell's blends. Caol Ila Hidden Malts are available at 12 years old (profiled), at 18 years old and at cask strength with no age statement. It is bottled as special vintages such as Caol Ila 1975 and in the Rare Malts series at 23 years old. Independent bottlings are also available in Gordon & MacPhail's Connoisseurs Choice range, Signatory and Cadenhead.

The visitor centre and shop are open all year, but appointments are advisable.

Feature	Profile
●●●	Body
●	Sweetness
●●●●	Smoky
●●	Medicinal
●	Tobacco
	Honey
●●	Spicy
	Winey
●●	Nutty
●	Malty
●	Fruity
●	Floral

Age 12 years
Strength 43%
Nose Smoky and spicy, a malty sweetness and a whiff of sea breeze
Taste Peat, pepper and cigar notes, with hints of nuts, lemons and cloves
Cluster J Full-bodied, dry, pungent, peaty and medicinal, with spicy, tobacco notes
Similar to Ardbeg, Talisker, Oban

CAOL ILA™

AGED **12** YEARS

ISLAY SINGLE MALT WHISKY

Out of sight, in a remote cove near Port Askaig lies Caol Ila, hidden gem among Islay's distilleries since 1846. Not easy to find, Caol Ila's secret malt is nonetheless highly prized among *devotees* of the Islay style.

Caol Ila Distillery, Port Askaig, Isle of Islay. lies here close to *Loch nam Ban*, source of its pure mash water. The sea provides and once brought steamers to collect a whisky appreciated for its ... lighter-bodied than many Islay malts, yet with all their typical pre...

70cl

CAPERDONICH

{*capper*-DON-*ich*}

Caperdonich distillery was built in 1898 by J & J Grant, across the road from Glen Grant, and was originally known as Glen Grant Number Two. It is named after the Caperdonich Spring, a source it shares with Glen Grant, and the intention was to extend the production capacity of Glen Grant, which was greatly in demand during the Victorian boom years. The two distilleries were originally connected by a pipe high above the road, known locally as the "whisky pipe", hence Rothes residents boasted that their streets flowed with whisky.

The distillery's success was short-lived, however, as it suffered from the industry recession following the Pattison crash, closing in 1902 after 5 years' operation. It remained closed for over 60 years, but was rebuilt and extended in 1965–67 to a functional 1960s design capable of being run by just 2 men. The distillery uses lightly peated malted barley, and operates a copper-domed mash tun, 8 stainless steel washbacks and 4 stills. The stills are now connected to modern cylindrical condensers, but the original Victorian copper worm tub condensers are still visible outside, and the malting chimney, minus pagoda roof, has been retained. The whisky is mostly matured in American ex-bourbon refill casks at the Burnfoot warehouse site nearby.

Caperdonich Single Speyside Malt whisky is available at 16 years old (profiled), cask strength non chill-filtered. Other editions are in Gordon & MacPhail's Connoisseurs Choice range at 1980 and 1968 vintages, and from Cadenhead at 14 and 23 years old. Cadenhead also supply Caperdonich at 24 years old cask strength from a sherry butt, a stunning malt.

Feature	Profile
●	Body
●●	Sweetness
●	Smoky
	Medicinal
	Tobacco
●	Honey
●●	Spicy
	Winey
●	Nutty
●●	Malty
●●	Fruity
●●●	Floral

Age 16 years
Strength 55.8%
Nose Oaky vanilla, pear drops, summer meadows and sweet peas
Taste Light bodied, medium sweet, mangoes, cloves, almonds, or nougat notes, and a hint of smoke
Cluster E Light, medium sweet, low peat, with floral, malty notes and fruity, spicy, honey hints
Similar to Glenlossie, Glenburgie, Braeval

- CHIVAS BROTHERS -
CASK STRENGTH EDITION
NON CHILL-FILTERED
Single Speyside Malt Scotch Whisky

Caperdonich

Aged **16** YEARS   Batch No.   **CD 16 001**

Bottled straight from the cask at **55.8** % vol.

Distilled **1988** | Bottled **2005**   Contents **50cl.**

Bottled in Scotland by Chivas Brothers Ltd., Distillers, Keith, AB55 5BS | Sample

PRODUCT OF SCOTLAND

CHIVAS BROTHERS DISTILLERS, KEITH-CASK STRENGTH EDITION

Batch No. CD 16 001

CARDHU

{*car*-DOO}

ardhu is Gaelic for "Black Rock". The distillery, originally named Cardow, was one of the first to be licensed. This took place in 1824, following about ten years' operation as an illicit whisky still. The founders were John Cumming, a farmer, and his wife Helen, who would fly a red flag from the barn to warn other crofters when the Excise men were searching for illicit stills. On the basis of Helen Cumming's active involvement, Cardhu claims to be the only distillery to be pioneered by a woman. Female emancipation at Cardhu did not end with Helen, however, as the Cummings' daughter-in-law Elizabeth took charge when her husband Lewis died in 1872, rebuilding it in 1885 on the present site and extending it further in 1887. For her enterprise and industry, Elizabeth Cumming was known as the "Queen of the Whisky Trade".

Cardhu Single Malt was the world's fastest-growing single malt whisky when in 2003, it became the focus of a major row for being re-launched without consultation, and with its packaging virtually unchanged, as a 'pure malt'. This comprised a blend of whiskies from more than one distillery, aimed at satisfying the rampant demand for Cardhu. Other distillers objected to a blend of whiskies being marketed under the name of an individual distillery, arging that the term "pure" was imprecise and could confuse consumers. In the event, Diageo backed down and re-introduced Cardhu single malt in July 2005.

Its water is drawn from springs on Mannoch Hill, and peat for the distillery was originally cut from Dallas Moor. Today, Cardhu operates a computer-controlled mash tun, 8 Scottish larch washbacks and 6 swan-necked stills. The whisky is matured in warehouses at the distillery, using only ex-bourbon American oak casks, either butts or hogsheads, which explains its light, delicate character.

Cardhu Single Malt is only available at 12 years old (profiled) and is an important component in the Johnnie Walker blends.

The visitor centre and shop are open all year, offering guided tours and tastings. Visitors may even meet the distillery ghost, a former worker who evidently didn't want to leave!

Feature	Profile
●	Body
●●●	Sweetness
●	Smoky
	Medicinal
	Tobacco
●	Honey
●	Spicy
	Winey
●●	Nutty
●●	Malty
●●	Fruity
●●	Floral

Age 12 years
Strength 40%
Nose Fragrant, fruity and sweet
Taste Some spice, fruit, nuts and hint of smoke. Quite sweet and fresh
Cluster D Light, medium-sweet, low or no peat, with fruity, floral, malty notes and nutty hints
Similar to Arran, Aultmore, Speyside

CLYNELISH

{KLINE-*leash*}

Clynelish is Sutherland's only distillery and the second most northerly of the Scottish mainland. It was established in 1819 by the Marquis of Stafford, later the first Duke of Sutherland, as an outlet for cheap grain from his tenant farms during the Highland clearances. Its location was also chosen for its proximity to Brora coal field, which had operated since the 16th century. As such it was one of the first purpose-built distilleries, with 1 wash still and 1 spirit still, commencing production in 1821. In the mid-nineteenth century the distillery was improved and extended by George Lawson who, with his sons, combined running the distillery with farming for 50 years. During his visit in 1886, Alfred Barnard reported that Clynelish whisky was highly prized and the distillery supplied only private customers throughout the kingdom. The recession of 1931 forced Clynelish to close, full production not recommencing until the end of World War II. Electricity replaced coal at Clynelish in the 1960s

and, in 1968, a new distillery was added next door with a copper-domed mash tun, 8 Oregon pine washbacks and 6 large stills. At just under 40 years old, Clynelish is one of the youngest distilleries on the map, and it was selected as one of Diageo's 'Hidden Malts' in 2002.

The team at Clynelish claim to produce their own genuine brand of liquid gold, as the water drawn from nearby Clynemilton Burn runs over veins of gold on its way down Colbheinn. The two distilleries operated alongside each other until 1983, when the original one was closed. The whisky from the original distillery is sold as "Brora", available in Diageo's Rare Malts range at 20 years old and in vintages such as 1973, 1974 and 1982. Clynelish Single Malt whisky is available at 14 years old (profiled) and at 23 years old in Diageo's Rare Malts range. Other vintage editions are available from Gordon & MacPhail and Signatory. The current Clynelish malts are far less peaty than Brora and earlier

Clynelish versions. The label features a Scottish wildcat, which is the emblem of Sutherland.

Visitors can be assured of a warm welcome at the distillery, which offers tours and tastings from March to October. Combine a tour of Clynelish distillery with a round of golf, salmon and trout fishing on Loch Shin, or a visit to Dunrobin Castle, the ancestral seat of the Dukes of Sutherland.

Feature	Profile
●●●	Body
●●	Sweetness
●	Smoky
	Medicinal
●	Tobacco
●●	Honey
●●●	Spicy
	Winey
●	Nutty
●●	Malty
●●	Fruity
●●●	Floral

Age 14 years
Strength 46%
Nose Fragrant, perfumed with citric fruits, spicy and a thread of smoke
Taste Full-bodied, creamy malt with fruit and spice to the fore, mustard and tobacco
Cluster C Medium-bodied, medium-sweet, with fruity, floral, honey, malty notes and spicy hints
Similar to Glen Ord, Balvenie, Benriach

CRAGGANMORE

{*Crag-an*-MOOR}

Cragganmore was established in 1869 by "Big" John Smith, one of the most experienced of Victorian distillers, who was responsible for starting and running several distilleries throughout Scotland. He chose the site for its plentiful supply of cold, spring water cascading down nearby Craggan Mor and for its close proximity to the Great Highland Railway line.

The distillery is constructed from greenstone, quarried from Craggan Mor, and it lies on a sweeping bend of the river Spey beside the former railway line, which is now part of the Speyside Way. Indeed, Cragganmore was one of the first to use "whisky specials" – long trains, heading south, with thousands of gallons of whisky aboard.

The water source is the Craggan Burn, and the distillery operates a modern copper-domed Lauter mash tun, 6 Oregon pine washbacks and 4 stills. Instead of the more usual swan necks, the two spirit stills are flat-topped with T-shaped lyne arms. These increase reflux such that the heavier vapours fall back and only the lighter alcohols pass to the condensers. Cragganmore has also unusually retained traditional copper worm-tub condensers, which result in higher catalysis due to longer contact of the vapours with copper. The resulting spirit is light and delightfully floral. The whisky is matured mainly in American oak ex-bourbon casks, in traditional dunnage warehouses.

Cragganmore Single Highland Malt 12 years old is Diageo's "Classic" Speysider, one of their six Classic Malts. It is also available at 10 and 29 years old, and in limited editions, such as a 1991 vintage double-matured Distillers Edition finished in port casks; and Cragganmore 1993 vintage, which is

Feature	Profile
●●	Body
●●	Sweetness
●●	Smoky
	Medicinal
●	Tobacco
●●	Honey
●●	Spicy
●	Winey
●●	Nutty
●●	Malty
●	Fruity
●●●●	Floral

Age 12 years
Strength 40%
Nose Rich, medium-sweet, fragrant and flowery, with notes of herbs and smoke
Taste Medium-bodied, firm, very floral, malty with touches of peat, honey and spice
Cluster B Medium-bodied, medium-sweet, with nutty, malty, floral, honey and fruity notes
Similar to Benromach, Blair Athol, Glenturret

heavily sherried, having been solely matured in European Bodega sherry casks.

Visitors are welcomed from July to September by appointment, for tours and tastings. These end in the "Cragganmore Club", a converted private drawing room of a Victorian sporting lodge, where there is an exhibition of Cragganmore artefacts.

CRAIGELLACHIE

{*craig*-ELL-*ach*-*ee*}

The village of Craigellachie beside the Spey boasts three landmarks – Thomas Telford's elegant single-span iron bridge completed in 1814; the Craigellachie Hotel with its famous Quaich Bar stocking almost 600 malt whiskies; and the distillery, which surveys the scene from a spur jutting out of the Rock of Craigellachie. It was built in 1891 by "restless" Peter Mackie and Alexander Edward, rebuilt in 1896, and extended in 1965, and its whisky has long been used as the heart of White Horse blends. The distillery's Victorian pagoda-topped chimney survives, but its stillroom is of modern construction, dating from 1965.

Craigellachie draws its process water from springs on Little Conval, and uses lightly peated malted barley supplied to order. It operates a large stainless steel Lauter mash tun, 8 Oregon pine washbacks and 4 large stills. The mash tun is one of the most technically advanced in the industry, with continuous sparging by which hot water is added continuously rather than in the traditional 3 batches. The arms move up and down while rotating and use a combination of rakes and blades to ensure maximum extraction of sugars. Craigellachie is one of the few distilleries to have retained traditional copper worm condensers. These create a richer spirit with more character due to the high contact the vapours have with copper, resulting in more catalysis. The whisky is matured in ex-bourbon American oak casks and a few European oak sherry butts. Criagellachie was sold with the Dewar's portfolio to Bacardi in 1998, hence its malt whisky was distilled by the previous owners. They used lightly-peated barley to give the whisky a slightly smoky note.

The current single malt was first bottled in 2004 and features Telford's Bridge over the Spey as its emblem.

Craigellachie Single Speyside Malt whisky is available at 14 years old (profiled), and in Gordon and MacPhail's Connoisseurs Choice at vintages such as 1988. The whisky is used in Dewar's White Label, Dewar's Special Reserve 12 years old, and Ancestor de Luxe blends, which account for the bulk of its production. The malt is difficult to find, but is stocked at Dewar's World of Whisky in Aberfeldy.

There is no visitor centre, but

Feature	Profile
●●	Body
●●●	Sweetness
●●	Smoky
●	Medicinal
	Tobacco
	Honey
●	Spicy
	Winey
●●	Nutty
●●	Malty
●●	Fruity
●●	Floral

Age 14 years
Strength 40%
Nose Fragrant, flowery and smoky
Taste Sweet, smoky and creamy, with citrus, nuts and malty notes, some liquorice and a hint of spice
Cluster H Medium-bodied, medium-sweet, with smoky, fruity, spicy notes and floral, nutty hints
Similar to Balblair, Glenmorangie, Strathmill

SINGLE MALT SCOTCH WHISKY
Craigellachie
SPEYSIDE
1891

CRAIGELLACHIE DISTILLERY was founded in 1891 by a partnership formed by a group of BLENDERS and WHISKY MERCHANTS. The Distillery stands on the spur of a hill, overlooking the precipitous ROCK OF CRAIGELLACHIE, THE RIVER SPEY and THOMAS TELFORD's elegant single span Iron Bridge of 1815.

AGED **14** YEARS

70cl 40% vol

DISTILLED AND BOTTLED IN SCOTLAND
CRAIGELLACHIE DISTILLERY,
CRAIGELLACHIE, ABERLOUR.
FROM THE HOUSE OF DEWAR.

DAILUAINE

{*dal-*YOO-*in*}

Dailuaine distillery was founded by William Mackenzie in 1851, and its name is Gaelic for "the green vale". The distillery nestles in a pretty spot beside the Carron Burn, between Ben Rinnes and the River Spey. Its granite buildings are late-Victorian, and are nicely preserved despite a major fire in 1917. Until the 1950s the distillery was powered by an ingenious combination of two water wheels, coupled by an overhead chain, and four steam engines.

For more than a century, Dailuaine received its supplies and despatched its whisky by rail. The steam locomotive *Dailuaine No. 1* was in use until 1967 and is still preserved as a feature at Aberfeldy distillery in Perthshire. The distillery was converted to electricity in the 1950s and now operates 6 pot stills using natural gas steam heating.

Dailuaine draws its process water for mashing from the Bailliemullich Burn, and cooling water from the Carron Burn, all of which are fed by springs from Ben Rinnes. The emblem on the label is a badger, because badger setts are to be found in the woods nearby.

The whisky is matured in a combination of bourbon and sherry casks. Most is used in Johnnie Walker blends, though the 16 years old Dailuaine Single Malt (profiled) is available in Diageo's Flora and Fauna series, in Gordon and MacPhail's Connoisseurs Choice range vintage 1975 and from Adelphi and Signatory.

Dailuaine does not have a visitor centre or offer tours.

Feature	Profile
●●●●	Body
●●	Sweetness
●●	Smoky
	Medicinal
	Tobacco
●	Honey
●●	Spicy
●●	Winey
●●	Nutty
●●	Malty
●●	Fruity
●	Floral

Age 16 years
Strength 43%
Nose Fruity and aromatic, quite sherried and malty
Taste Full-bodied, barley sugar and autumn fruits, with vanilla, smoky and spicy notes
Cluster A Full-bodied, medium-sweet, pronounced sherry with fruity, spicy, malty notes and nutty, smoky hints
Similar to Royal Lochnagar, Dalmore, Glendronach

SPEYSIDE
SINGLE MALT SCOTCH WHISKY

DAILUAINE

In the GAELIC for "the green vale". The *distillery*, established in 1852, lies in a hollow by the *CARRON BURN* in *BANFFSHIRE*. This *Single Malt Scotch Whisky* has a *full bodied fruity* nose and a smoky finish. For more than a *hundred years* all *distillery supplies* were despatched by *rail*. The *steam locomotive* "DAILUAINE NO.1" was in use from 1939–1967 and is *preserved* on the *STRATHSPEY RAILWAY*.

AGED **16** YEARS

DALMORE

{*dall*-MORE}

Dalmore is Norse for "big meadowland" and the distillery was built in 1839 by Alexander Matheson in fine barley growing country, on the site of a former meal mill. It sits in a beautiful spot opposite the Black Isle – not actually an island, but a peninsula of the Cromarty Firth. The area is teeming with wildlife, with porpoises in the Firth, a buzzard's nest in the firs, and herons on the shore. Many original Victorian buildings remain, with the pagoda-topped malting kiln as a centrepiece, though in 1966 the distillery was extended. In World War I it was requisitioned by the Americans for the production of deep sea mines, and they added the "Yankie" pier. Another feature is a Victorian steam engine from 1898.

The emblem on the label features the stag's head of the Mackenzie clan, as the Mackenzie whisky family owned Dalmore for over 80 years from 1874. Legend has it that Alexander III awarded the stag's head to the clan when Mackenzie saved him from a charging wounded stag. Dalmore whisky is favoured in cigar-smoking circles, so a "Cigar Malt" was produced to foster this association. It is also an excellent "after-dinner" malt.

The distillery draws soft clear water from the River Alness, which flows from Loch Morie below Ben Wyvis. It operates a stainless steel mash tun, 8 Oregon pine washbacks, 2 large and 2 small wash stills encased in copper cooling jackets to increase reflux, and 2 large and 2 small flat-topped spirit stills. Production is quite high, most of which goes for blending. The whisky is matured in a mixture of first fill ex-bourbon American oak and specially selected aged oloroso sherry casks, stored in warehouses at the site and married in sherry butts prior to bottling.

The Dalmore Highland Malt Scotch whisky is available at 12 years old (profiled) and at 21 and 30 years old, and as a "Cigar Malt", which has won awards at the Habanos Cigar Festival in Cuba. There are also special editions,

Feature	Profile
●●●	Body
●●	Sweetness
●●	Smoky
●	Medicinal
	Tobacco
●	Honey
●●	Spicy
●●	Winey
●	Nutty
●●	Malty
●●●	Fruity
●	Floral

Age 12 years
Strength 40%
Nose Rich, fruity and sherried, with a nutty, orange/marzipan note and a whiff of smoke
Taste Medium-bodied, malt and marmalade, with some peat and sherry notes and a hint of salt
Cluster A Full-bodied, medium-sweet, pronounced sherry with fruity, spicy, malty notes and nutty, smoky hints
Similar to Royal Lochnagar, Dailuaine, Glendronach

such as a Dalmore 1973 Vintage Gonzalez Byass sherry cask finish and a vintage 50 years old limited edition. Dalmore whiskies have won numerous awards at international spirits festivals.

The visitor centre is open all year. It has a shop and offers a video presentation, tours and tastings.

DALWHINNIE

{dal-WHIN-*ee}*

Dalwhinnie is Gaelic for "meeting place", and stands at a point on an old Highland road where cattle drovers would meet and rest. The distillery was built by Alexander Mackenzie in 1897 and started production in 1898, only to close almost immediately. Its location – a "desolate, wind-sliced, rain-lashed patch of Highland wilderness"– was chosen for the abundant supply of clear, Highland spring water, ample peat for the fire, and its proximity to the Highland Railway line.

The distillery was sold several times before 1926, when it was acquired by the Distillers Company, now part of Diageo. It was rebuilt in 1938 following a major fire, modernised in the 1970s and refurbished in the 1990s when a visitor centre was added. The 1930s stone buildings are white-faced with slate roofs and twin pagoda-topped chimneys, set against a stark backdrop of the snow-capped heather hills of Drumochter Pass and the Athol Forest. It is certainly Scotland's highest distillery and probably the coldest too.

It doubles as a Met Office weather station and in 1994 recorded the lowest average temperature of any inhabited part of Britain at 6° C.

Its snow-melted water collects at 2,000 feet (610 metres) in Lochan an Doire-Uaine and then runs through peat and purple heather into the distillery burn, Allt an t'Sluic. In earlier times the barley was malted over a fire of locally-cut peat, but today it is supplied lightly peated to order. The distillery operates a stainless steel mash tun, 1 Oregon pine and 5 Siberian larch washbacks, and 2 large onion-shaped stills. Somewhat unusually, the spirit is still condensed in traditional copper worms housed in large wooden tubs at the front of the still house (right of picture). The whisky is matured in ex-bourbon American oak casks, taking longer than normal due to the altitude and humidity.

Dalwhinnie Single Highland Malt is available at 15 years old (profiled) in Diageo's Classic Malts range, and in limited editions such as a double-matured Distillers' Edition 1990 vintage finished in oloroso sherry casks, and at

csak strength aged 29 and 36 years old. Richard Joynson, of Loch Fyne Whiskies, described it as "exotic white lingerie (pure, with a distinctly racy streak)". Indeed an earlier label declared it "an elegant malt whisky with a heathery, lacy finish", and it is an excellent accompaniment to rich desserts such as a black forest gâteau or sticky toffee pudding and cream (enough said).

The visitor centre is open all year and attracts 30,000 visitors annually and offers tours, tastings and a shop.

Feature	Profile
●●	Body
●●	Sweetness
●●	Smoky
	Medicinal
	Tobacco
●●	Honey
●	Spicy
	Winey
●	Nutty
●●	Malty
●●	Fruity
●●	Floral

Age 15 years
Strength 43%
Nose Sweet, nutty aroma with a floral edge hinting of smoke and marmalade
Taste Fresh and heathery, citrus fruits, honey, vanilla and a whiff of peat
Cluster C Medium-bodied, medium-sweet, with fruity, floral, honey, malty notes and spicy hints
Similar to Benriach, Glen Elgin, Glen Ord

DEANSTON

{DEANS-*ton*}

maturation warehouse. The water that supplies the distillery and drives its turbines is diverted from the Teith by a canal, and returned to the river through a network of Victorian water caverns that are home to a colony of bats.

Deanston distillery draws its water from the river Teith and uses un-peated malted barley, though the mashing water contains enough peaty traces to account for a slightly smoky note in the finished whisky. It operates a large open cast iron mash tun, 8 stainless steel washbacks and 4 medium sized pot stills. The whisky is matured in a range of American and European oak refill casks, and also some fresh sherry butts that will contribute more winey flavours to future versions.

Deanston Single Highland Malt whisky is available at 12 years old (profiled), and at 17 years old. Special vintage editions are also produced,

Deanston distillery was originally a cotton mill, built in 1785 by Richard Arkwright who invented the "spinning jenny", and several of its buildings date from that period. It lies beside the river Teith near Castle Doune in Perthshire. The mill was originally driven by water power, but it was converted to a distillery in 1965, which is powered by hydro-electric turbines that also contribute surplus electricity to the national grid. It retains some interesting listed buildings, including a magnificent vaulted weaving shed now used as a

such as a cask-strength single malt aged 30 years. The whisky is also used in the company's Scottish Leader and Black Bottle blends, in Drumgray Highland Cream Liqueur, which won gold medals in 1993 and 1999, and Wallace Single Malt Scotch Whisky Liqueur.

Deanston does not have a visitor centre.

Feature	Profile
●●	Body
●●	Sweetness
●	Smoky
	Medicinal
	Tobacco
●●	Honey
●	Spicy
●	Winey
●	Nutty
●●●	Malty
●●	Fruity
●	Floral

Age 12 years
Strength 40%
Nose Fragrant and honeyed with a malty, cereal note
Taste Malty and fruity, with a hint of spice and a sweet aftertaste
Cluster F Medium-bodied, medium-sweet, low peat, malty notes and sherry, honey, spicy hints
Similar to Ardmore, Auchroisk, Glenrothes

DUFFTOWN

{DUFF-*ton*}

Dufftown distillery was converted from a meal mill in 1896 by Peter MacKenzie and Richard Stackpole. It is a pretty Victorian stone distillery nestling in rolling hills and woodland beside the River Dullan, a subsidiary of the Spey. The distillery's emblem is a kingfisher, and examples of these can be seen fishing for trout nearby.

Its water is drawn from Highland John's Well, an excellent source of pure spring water that rises in the Conval Hills about four miles from the distillery, and which has never been known to fail, even in the driest summer. The ownership of the well was initially hotly disputed, to the extent that rival distillers would venture out in the dead of night to divert and re-divert its course, but this was eventually decided in Dufftown's favour early in the twentieth century.

The distillery was extended in 1968, in 1980 and again in 1999 to its present capacity. It now operates a stainless steel mash tun, 12 stainless steel washbacks and 6 stills, using a complex distillation that is capable of producing over 4 million litres (7 million pints) of spirit a year. The single malt is matured in Spanish sherry and American bourbon casks, whereas refill casks are used for the whisky intended for blending.

Most of the production is used in Bell's 8 years old blend. The single malt is available in Diageo's Flora and Fauna range at 15 years old (profiled), and in the Rare Malts series as a 1975 vintage. It is also available at various vintages from Cadenhead, Murray McDavid and Signatory. Dufftown distillery does not have a visitor centre or offer tours.

Feature	Profile
●●	Body
●●●	Sweetness
●	Smoky
●	Medicinal
	Tobacco
	Honey
	Spicy
	Winey
●	Nutty
●●	Malty
●●	Fruity
●●	Floral

Age 15 years
Strength 43%
Nose Sweet, fragrant and fruity aroma
Taste Medium-bodied with flowers, fruit and treacle toffee flavours, and a hint of smoke
Cluster G Medium-bodied, sweet, low peat and floral notes
Similar to Glenfiddich, Miltonduff, Speyburn

HIGHLAND
SINGLE MALT *SCOTCH WHISKY*

DUFFTOWN

Distillery was established near *Dufftown* at the end of the 19th The bright flash of the KINGFISHER can often be seen over the *DULLAN RIVER*, which flows past the *old stone buildings* of the distillery on its way north to the *SPEY*. This *single HIGHLAND MALT WHISKY* is typically *SPEYSIDE* in character with a *delicate, fragrant, vibrant flowery* aroma and taste which *lingers* on the palate.

AGED **15** YEARS

EDRADOUR

{*edra*-DOWER}

Edradour is the classic example of a farm distillery, the smallest in Scotland and run by three men. If you want to see what whisky distillation was like in the nineteenth century, then this is it. Established in 1825 as a farmers' co-operative, the present buildings were constructed by the Duke of Athol and date from 1837. Little has changed here in the past 160 years, the last major modernisation being in 1947 when the water wheel was replaced by electricity.

Its water flows down granite hills and through the peat of Moulin Moor, before rising clear and cold a short distance above the distillery. Everything about Edradour is small. It operates a cast iron mash tun with a capacity of only one tonne of barley, 2 Oregon pine washbacks, and 2 tiny stills. The still

house is roughly the size of your living room, and the spirit still is the smallest allowed under Excise regulations – any smaller and it could be hidden away in a hillside; and indeed they were in the eighteenth century, as this is an area rich in smuggling lore. The output at Edradour is tiny too, distilling in a year what a typical Speyside distillery produces in a week. Edradour's biggest statistic is the number of visitors who flock here to experience the charm of a traditional farm distillery set in pretty gardens, and the warm welcome of the visitor centre staff, who outnumber the production team.

Edradour Single Highland Malt whisky is only available at 10 years old (profiled). It is a hand-crafted malt whisky, unique and difficult to find, but well worth the hunt. Special 'Straight

from the Cask' vintage Edradour Malts
have been finished in wine barrels that
previously contained Barolo, Bordeaux,
Burgundy, Chardonnay, Madiera,
Marsala, Port, Sauternes, and Sherry.
They are also available in limited
editions, such as Edradour 1983 vintage
finished in port pipes, and a Decanter
vintage 1993. For the latest position
visit *edradour.co.uk*

The visitor centre, a converted malt
barn, and shop are open all year. Tours
include an audio-visual presentation,
exhibition of traditional whisky-making,
and a free tasting.

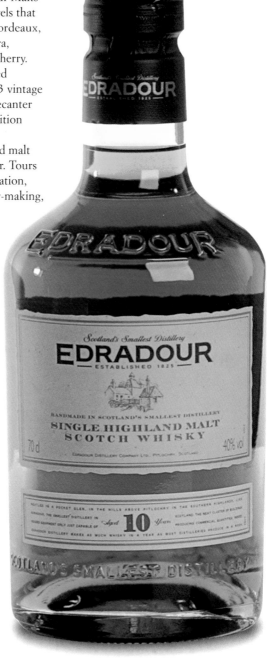

Feature	Profile
●●	Body
●●●	Sweetness
●	Smoky
	Medicinal
	Tobacco
●●	Honey
●	Spicy
●	Winey
●●●●	Nutty
●●	Malty
●●	Fruity
●●	Floral

Age 10 years
Strength 40%
Nose Fragrant and honeyed,
minty like sugared almonds,
with a whiff of smoke
Taste Sweet and creamy with
pistachio, fruit and malt notes,
and hints of sherry and spice
Cluster B Medium-bodied,
medium-sweet, with nutty,
malty, floral, honey and
fruity notes
Similar to Glencadam,
Strathisla, Longmorn

FETTERCAIRN

{FETTER-*care'n*}

Fettercairn distillery was founded in 1824 by Sir Alexander Ramsay on the site of a former corn mill in the beautiful rolling Mearns of Kincardineshire. This is my family's "local", as our first Laird was John Wischard of Pitarrow, Viscount of the Mearns, from about 1240. It was the second distillery to be licensed in Scotland, but illicit stills are believed to have been worked in the hills much earlier. The distillery was sold with Fasque House in 1830 to Sir John Gladstone, father of William Ewart Gladstone, who spent his early years here and went on to serve 4 terms as Prime Minister between 1868–1894. Gladstone greatly helped the industry by abolishing the hated malt tax and licensing glass whisky bottles. Queen Victoria and Prince Albert visited Fettercairn in 1861 during one of their Scottish tours, as commemorated by a fine arch in the town.

The distillery was rebuilt in 1890 after a fire and extended to 4 stills in 1966. It has pretty whitewashed Victorian stone buildings with a single pagoda chimney above the former malt barn.

It draws its water from the Cnoc Calma (Sturdy Hill) spring in the Grampian mountains, and uses lightly peated malted barley. It is a traditional distillery, operating a copper domed cast iron mash tun, 8 Oregon pine washbacks and 4 small pot stills. The spirit stills have unique waterfalls cascading down their necks to cool the vapours and increase reflux resulting in a lighter spirit. The whisky is matured in American oak bourbon casks, European oak sherry casks and refills, and stored in warehouses at the distillery, the oldest Fettercairn cask being 1962.

Fettercairn 1824 Single Highland Malt is available at 12 years old, and at 15 years old cask strength bottled at the distillery. It is also available in limited editions such as Stillman's Dram 30 years old and in Gordon & MacPhail's Connoisseurs Choice range. The whisky is used in many blends, notably Whyte and Mackay.

The visitor centre and shop are open between May and September, and offer an audio-visual presentation, distillery tours and tastings.

Feature	Profile
●	Body
●●	Sweetness
●●	Smoky
	Medicinal
●	Tobacco
●●	Honey
●●	Spicy
●	Winey
●●	Nutty
●●●	Malty
●	Fruity
●	Floral

Age 12 years
Strength 40%
Nose Rather sweet and malty, with a vanilla note and some spice
Taste Light bodied, creamy butterscotch, slightly smoky with hints of honey and nutmeg
Cluster F Medium-bodied, medium-sweet, low peat, malty notes and sherry, honey, spicy hints
Similar to Ardmore, Deanston, Tomatin

GLENALLACHIE

{*glen*-ALLACH-*ee*}

Glenallachie distillery was built in 1967 beside the Lour Burn above Aberlour by Charles Mackinlay & Co. to a functional design by the architect William Delmé Evans, and is typical of 1960s single level distillery architecture. The cooling water is drawn from ponds created by a dam in the river fed from a small waterfall, and this provides the distillery's most attractive feature. The warm water from the condensers is piped back to the ponds, which gives them a steamy look in winter and is enjoyed by a colony of ducks that are included in the inventory.

The distillery draws its water from deep granite springs and snow-fed burns on Ben Rinnes and uses lightly peated malted barley. It operates a stainless steel semi-Lauter mash tun, 6 stainless steel washbacks and 4 medium-sized pot stills. The wash stills have pinched waists while the spirit stills follow the more usual onion shape. The whisky is matured in ex-bourbon American oak casks and refills for blending, with a few sherry butts reserved for the single malt.

Glenallachie Single Malt Scotch whisky is available at 12 years old (profiled) from Delhaize in Belgium, matured in a regular bourbon cask. It is also available at cask strength, non chill-filtered 16 years old from Chivas Brothers, matured in a new sherry butt. These two editions are quite different, and illustrate the major influences of cask maturation and chill-filtration on

Feature	Profile
●	Body
●●●	Sweetness
●	Smoky
	Medicinal
	Tobacco
●	Honey
●	Spicy
	Winey
●	Nutty
●●	Malty
●●	Fruity
●●	Floral

Age 12 years
Strength 40%
Nose Aromatic, fresh and malty with a whiff of smoke
Taste Light but well-balanced, with floral, vanilla and apple notes, and a long sweet finish
Cluster E Light, medium-sweet, low peat, with floral, malty notes and fruity, spicy, honey hints
Similar to Allt á Bhainne, Glenburgie, Glenlossie

the same spirit. The new Chivas version was put in Cluster A by *Whisky Analyst*. Glenallachie malts can also be found as vintages in Gordon & MacPhail's Connoisseurs Choice range, and by Signatory and Douglas Laing. It is used in Clan Campbell 12 years old, Legendary 18 years old and White Heather blends.

Glenallachie distillery does not have a visitor centre or offer tours.

GLENBURGIE

{*ben*-RIN-*is*}

lenburgie distillery was first licensed to William Paul in 1829 as Kilnflats distillery, but it was founded in 1810. It was named Glenburgie in 1878 after 16th century Burgie Castle. In 1887, Alfred Barnard described it as "a very ancient distillery, and about as old-fashioned as it is possible to conceive". In the late 1930s the distillery was unusually managed by a woman, Miss Nicol. Very few women have aspired to such a position, the other exceptions being Helen and Elizabeth Cummings of Cardow, and Bessie Williamson of Laphroaig. The distillery is a stark contrast of ancient and modern, a completely new distillery having been built in the grounds of the original one in 2004. It nestles quietly in a wooded valley surrounded by typical Morayshire farmland, with salty air blowing in fresh from the Moray Firth. Some of its original Victorian stone buildings remain, including the manager's office, the excise office and a warehouse.

The malted barley is supplied to order with very light peating. The original distillery operated a traditional copper-domed mash tun, 13 wash backs (of which 6 were Oregon pine and 7 were stainless steel), and 4 conventional pot stills. It was extended in 1958, when floor malting ceased and 2 Lomond stills were added. These produced a rich, peaty Glencraig malt whisky that can still be found, but they were replaced with a pair of conventional stills in 1981.

The new distillery is ultra modern, to an ergonomic design on one floor, and operated by one man and a computer. It has a Lauter mash tun with continuous sparging, 12 stainless steel washbacks and the original 4 pot stills, which were refurbished and transferred from the old distillery. The process water is drawn from springs in the distillery's grounds and the cooling water comes from its own dam, fed by a stream. The whisky is matured in ex-bourbon barrels, mostly from Heaven Hill, Kentucky. Glenburgie used to claim to be part of Speyside's Glenlivet appellation, despite being located some

Feature	Profile
●	Body
●●	Sweetness
●	Smoky
	Medicinal
	Tobacco
●	Honey
●	Spicy
	Winey
●	Nutty
●●	Malty
●●	Fruity
●●●	Floral

Age 15 years
Strength 46%
Nose Fragrant, new mown hay, light and spirity
Taste Aperitif-style with toffee, treacle and vanilla, a short finish with a hint of smoke
Cluster E Light, medium-sweet, low peat, with floral, malty notes and fruity, spicy, honey hints
Similar to Caperdonich, Bunnahabhain, Glenallachie

50 miles from the Braes of Glenlivet. Glenburgie Single Malt is available at 15 years old in the Allied Distilleries series (profiled). It is also available in Gordon & MacPhail's Speyside Malt Range at 10 years old, and in certain vintages, such as 1964. Most of the production goes for blending, notably in Teacher's and Ballantines.

All the present malts were produced by the old distillery, but the new distillery's product is unlikely to be substantially different since great care has been taken to maintain the character of the spirit.

GLENCADAM

{*ben*-RIN-*is*}

Glencadam distillery was founded in the outskirts of Brechin in 1825, a year after the Excise Act of 1824 legalised large-scale distilling. The setting is the strikingly beautiful Strathmore vale of Sidlaw Hills. In former times the ancient sandstone city of Brechin had city walls and a magnificent medieval cathedral, built about 1150 and dedicated to St Ninian. It sits above the river Esk, and has witnessed many battles and historical events.

Alfred Barnard visited the distillery in 1886, and in the early 1900s Glencadam Highland Malt Whisky was a constituent of Gilmour Thomson's Royal Blend, a favourite of King Edward VII. In 1959 the distillery was modernised by Hiram Walker, but some of the original Victorian buildings have been retained, including the former Excise Officer's house now used as an office (pictured).

Brechin has since grown around the distillery, which is flanked on three sides by the cemetery, a retirement home and Brechin City football club.

The water source is the Moorans in Glen Esk, which flows from Moorfoot in the Grampian Hills. It operates a cast iron mash tun, 6 stainless steel washbacks and 2 small pot stills. The lyne arms from the stills unusually incline 15 degrees upwards, which encourages reflux. The whisky is matured in warehouses beside the distillery, in refill hogsheads, ex-bourbon barrels and a few European oak sherry casks.

Glencadam Single Highland Malt Whisky is available at 15 years old (profiled), and in the Allied Distilleries "Special Malts" series, also at 15 years old. It is also in Gordon & MacPhail's Connoisseurs Choice range and from Signatory and Cadenhead. Most of the production is used in blends such as Ballantine's and Stewart's Cream of the Barley.

It does not have a visitor centre, but visitors are welcome by appointment.

Feature	Profile
●●●	Body
●●●	Sweetness
●	Smoky
	Medicinal
	Tobacco
●●	Honey
	Spicy
●	Winey
●●●	Nutty
●	Malty
●●●	Fruity
●●	Floral

Age 15 years
Strength 40%
Nose Marzipan and vanilla, peaches and cream, and a whiff of smoke
Taste Medium-bodied, sweet and creamy, with pistachios, fruit salad and asparagus notes and aniseed in the finish
Cluster B Medium-bodied, medium-sweet, with nutty, malty, floral, honey and fruity notes
Similar to Edradour, Scapa, Knockando

GLEN DEVERON

{glen-DEV-er-en}

Macduff distillery was built in 1959 on the outskirts of Macduff, a small fishing town and seaside resort on the east bank of the River Deveron, opposite the ancient Royal burgh of Banff.

It draws its process water from springs above the distillery and its cooling water (when necessary) from the River Deveron, which gives its name to the malt whisky, although it can also be found as Macduff. Lightly peated, malted barley is delivered to order, and a mixture of distillers' culture and brewers' yeasts is used in the fermentation. The distillery operates a stainless steel mash tun, 9 stainless steel washbacks, 2 wash stills and 3 spirit stills. The whisky is matured in warehouses beside the Deveron in bourbon, sherry and refill casks, some of which are charred in the distillery's own cooperage to add toasty, vanilla flavours. Macduff was sold with the Dewar's portfolio to Bacardi in 1998, hence its Glen Deveron malt whisky was distilled by the previous owners.

Glen Deveron Single Highland Malt whisky is available at 10 years old (profiled), at 5 years old for export only, and as Macduff versions at vintage bottlings in Gordon & MacPhail's Connoisseurs Choice range, Cadenhead and Signatory. It is also used in William Lawson's Finest Scotch Whisky and 12 years old Scottish Gold blends.

Macduff distillery does not have a visitor centre or offer tours.

Aerial view of Macduff distillery beside the River Deveron, home of Glen Deveron Malt and William Lawson's blends.

Feature	Profile
●●	Body
●●●	Sweetness
●	Smoky
●	Medicinal
●	Tobacco
●	Honey
●	Spicy
●●	Winey
	Nutty
●●	Malty
	Fruity
●	Floral

Age 10 years
Strength 40%
Nose Fresh, sweet and malty, with a sherry note and a hint of sea air
Taste Medium-bodied, honey and spice notes, some oaky vanilla and a soft smoky finish
Cluster F Medium-bodied, medium-sweet, low peat, malty notes and sherry, honey, spicy hints
Similar to Tomatin, Glenrothes, Tullibardine

GLENDRONACH

{*glen*-DRON-*ach*}

Glendronach is Gaelic for "valley of the blackberries". It is a small distillery nestling in the Valley of Forgue by the town of Huntly, a converted meal mill adjacent to Glen House, which dates from 1771. The distillery was first licensed to James Allardice in 1826, but they had probably been distilling whisky here previously, as was common in mansion houses throughout Scotland in the 18th century. There is a charming tale of Allardice, while promoting his "Guid Glendronach" in Edinburgh, being drawn into the company of two prostitutes who greatly enjoyed his whisky and helped establish its "guid" reputation in the pubs along the Royal Mile. Alfred Barnard described the distillery in 1887 as "quaint and picturesque" being powered solely by two water-wheels, its water drawn from the Dronac Burn, which "although tinged with a golden brown, is also bright and perfectly clear".

Prior to 2005 the stills were coal-fired, and barley was turned by hand on the malting floor and dried in a pagoda-topped malt kiln over a peat fire. Today the malt is supplied un-peated to order and the stills are steam-heated, but the whisky dates from the previous operation that had remained unchanged since Barnard's visit. Indeed, Glendronach oozes tradition, with an atmosphere of timeless industry and family contentment.

The original buildings surround an old cobbled courtyard, and a welcome is assured from the resident rooks. Legend has it, that so long as the rooks remain, Glendronach will enjoy good fortune – for in the old days, it was the rooks that warned of approaching Excise officers!

The distillery operates a copper-domed cast iron mash tun, 9 traditional Oregon pine washbacks, and 4 original squat copper stills. The whisky is matured in traditional dunnage warehouses, in ex-

Feature	Profile
●●●	Body
●●	Sweetness
●●	Smoky
	Medicinal
	Tobacco
●●	Honey
●	Spicy
●●●	Winey
●●	Nutty
●●	Malty
●●●	Fruity
●	Floral

Age 12 years
Strength 40%
Nose Rich sherried aroma, some vanilla and nutty notes, and a whiff of smoke
Taste Full and complex flavour with dried fruits and malty-toffee notes, or tart oranges with honey, and a long creamy finish
Cluster A Full-bodied, medium-sweet, pronounced sherry with fruity, spicy, malty notes and nutty, smoky hints
Similar to Royal Lochnagar, Macallan, Dalmore

bourbon hogsheads and European oak butts. The immense flavour of the 15 years old single malt whisky derives from its long maturation in specially selected Spanish sherry casks, but this has been subtly modified in the new Glendronach 12 years old malt due to finishing in ex-bourbon barrels. It is also available at 33 years old in a presentation box, and as a 1968 vintage.

The distillery offers guided tours all year, a video presentation and a shop. Overnight accommodation is available.

GLENDULLAN

{*glen*-DULL-*an*}

Old Glendullan distillery was built in Dufftown in 1897 by William Williams and Sons. It was the seventh distillery to be built in Dufftown, and thus was coined the local saying "Rome was built of seven hills and Dufftown stands on seven stills".

All its machinery was powered by a 14ft (4.3 metres) water wheel driven by water from the River Fiddich, until after World War II. *Harper's Weekly* reported in 1897 that "This water power will be a great saving compared to steam engines". A private railway line, linked to Dufftown Station and shared with its sister distillery Mortlach, was used to deliver supplies and despatch the whisky to Aberdeen.

Distillation commenced in April 1898, the whisky being used initially for the Williams' blends. In 1902 Glendullan whisky became a favourite of King Edward

VII and, in 1995, it was chosen for the "Houses of Parliament" exclusive single malt by the then Speaker, Betty Boothroyd.

A modern distillery was added in 1972 next to "Old Glendullan", and for a while they ran in tandem. The new design, which was successfully repeated at several other distilleries, is unattractive but proved to be much more efficient and so the old distillery ceased production in 1985 and is now used for engineering work.

Glendullan distillery draws its process water from Goatswell Spring and its cooling water from the River Fiddich. It operates a 12 tonne copper-topped mash tun, 8 Oregon pine washbacks and 6 stills. The spirit stills are larger than the wash stills, which is rather unusual. The whisky is matured in oak refill casks, the bulk of its production now being used in Dewars, Bell's, Johnnie Walker and Old Parr blends.

Glendullan Single Malt whisky is available in the Diageo's Flora and Fauna range at 12 years old (profiled), at 8 years old, and as Glendullan

Feature	Profile
●●●	Body
●●	Sweetness
●	Smoky
	Medicinal
	Tobacco
●●	Honey
●	Spicy
●●	Winey
●	Nutty
●●	Malty
●●●	Fruity
●●	Floral

Age 12 years
Strength 43%
Nose Fruity, malty and honeyed with hints of sherry and vanilla oak
Taste Firm and mellow with fruity, honey and malty notes and a floral finish
Cluster C Medium-bodied, medium-sweet, with fruity, floral, honey, malty notes and spicy hints
Similar to Glen Ord, Balvenie, Glenlivet

Centenary, 16 years old cask strength edition non chill-filtered, which was specially bottled for Glendullan's centenary. Other vintages are available from Signatory and Cadenhead.

It does not have a visitor centre.

SPEYSIDE
SINGLE MALT
SCOTCH WHISKY

GLENDULLAN

distillery, located in a beautiful *wooded valley was* ⅍ built in 1897 and is one of seven *established* in *Dufftown* in the C19th. The *River Fiddich* flows past the *distillery*; originally *providing power* to drive machinery, it is now used ⅍ for cooling. *GLENDULLAN* is a firm, mellow *single MALT SCOTCH WHISKY* with a fruity bouquet and a smooth *lingering* finish.

AGED **12** YEARS

Distilled & Bottled in SCOTLAND
GLENDULLAN DISTILLERY
Dufftown, Keith, Banffshire, Scotland

43% vol   70cl

GLEN ELGIN

{glen-ELG-in}

Glen Elgin distillery was built near Elgin in 1898 by William Simpson and James Carle, and to a design by the architect Charles Doig. It commenced production in May 1900. The recession in the whisky industry, which followed that year, meant this was the last distillery to be built on Speyside for sixty years. The site was originally chosen for its proximity to Glen Burn and Longmorn station. The distillery was lit by paraffin and powered by water until electricity was installed in the 1950s. It draws its water from springs below Millbuies Loch.

Glen Elgin was rebuilt in 1964, with a new mash house and still house, and steam heating replaced the coal-fired boilers in 1970. It uses unpeated malted barley and uses a stainless steel Lauter mash tun, 6 larch washbacks and 6 onion shaped stills. The spirit is condensed in traditional copper worm tubs, and the resulting higher catalysis with the copper gives the whisky its signature floral note. An added bonus for the staff are fresh water shrimp which thrive in the tubs. The whisky is matured in American oak bourbon casks, refills, and a few European ex-sherry casks.

Glen Elgin Single Malt is available at 12 years old (profiled) in Diageo's Flora and Fauna range, in the Hidden Malts series at 12 years old, and as a vintage Glen Elgin 1971 in the Rare Malts range. It is the heart of White Horse and Bell's Extra Special blends, which take 95 per cent of its production. The emblem on the bottle is the house martin, because several pairs faithfully

Six traditional condensers, consisting of a copper worm immersed in a tub of cold running water, are still in use at Glen Elgin distillery.

Feature	Profile
●●	Body
●●●	Sweetness
●	Smoky
	Medicinal
	Tobacco
●●	Honey
●	Spicy
●	Winey
●	Nutty
●	Malty
●●	Fruity
●●●	Floral

Age 12 years
Strength 43%
Nose Honeyed and grassy with a whiff of smoke
Taste Aromatic and fresh with a tart fruitiness, vanilla and malty notes, and a hint of cloves
Cluster C Medium-bodied, medium-sweet, with fruity, floral, honey, malty notes and spicy hints
Similar to Glenlivet, Dalwhinnie, Linkwood

return every year to raise their young under the eaves of the distillery buildings. The distillery does not have a visitor centre or offer tours.

GLENFARCLAS

{*glen*-FAR-*class*}

Glenfarclas distillery, in the "valley of the green grass".

Glenfarclas distillery in Speyside is one of the few to have remained in private ownership since it was founded in 1836 by Robert Hay. Six generations of the Grant family have distilled whisky here. Glenfarclas means "the valley of the green grass". The distillery stands in beautiful, rolling meadows, drawing its soft water from the Green Burn that flows from Ben Rinnes over granite and through heather into the valley.

The distillery was rebuilt in 1897 and further extended and modernised in the 1960s. It operates a stainless steel Lauter mash tun, 12 stainless steel washbacks and 6 stills. The stills are amongst the largest on Speyside, with the big wash still holding nearly 30,000 litres.

Glenfarclas malt whiskies are now aged mainly in oloroso sherry casks, using a mixture of first-fill and refill, although this has not always been the case. This contributes to the malt's pronounced sherry character, particularly in the younger malts where new sherry casks have been used.

Glenfarclas Single Highland Malt Whisky is available at 10 years old (profiled) and at 12, 15, 17, 21, 25, 30, 40 and 50 years old and as a 10 years old cask-strength "105" malt whisky. The extensive range of Glenfarclas

The distillery workforce of 1891.

malts allows for detailed research on the effects of cask maturation.

Glenfarclas visitor centre features the splendid "Ships Room", which is fitted out with the original oak panelling and ship's furniture of the *Empress of Australia*, 1913–52. The visitor centre and shop are open all year for tours and tastings, and for connoiseurs there is a special tutored nosing and tasting if booked in advance.

Feature	Profile
●●	Body
●●●●	Sweetness
●	Smoky
	Medicinal
	Tobacco
●	Honey
●●	Spicy
●●●	Winey
●●	Nutty
●●●	Malty
●●	Fruity
●●	Floral

Age 10 years
Strength 40%
Nose Light, sweet and malty, with a floral, fruity nose
Taste Sweetly sherried with a creamy, nutty flavour and showing some spice and fruit
Cluster B Medium-bodied, medium-sweet, with nutty, malty, floral, honey and fruity notes
Similar to Glenturret, Blair Athol, Strathisla

GLENFIDDICH

{glen-FID-ich}

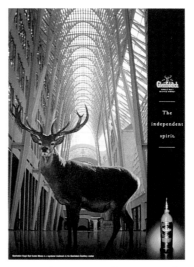

Glenfiddich is Gaelic for "valley of the deer". The distillery, which was founded in 1886 by William and Elizabeth Grant, started production on Christmas Day 1887 and has been continuously owned and managed by the Grant family for five generations.

All the water used at Glenfiddich, from mashing to bottling, is drawn from a single source – the Robbie Dhu Spring – hence their maxim "a single source of inspiration" and their claim to be the "château-bottled" malt whisky of Scotland. The distillery uses lightly-peated malted barley and operates 2 stainless steel mash tuns, 24 Douglas fir washbacks, 10 wash stills and 18 spirit stills.

The spirit stills are unusually small, being faithful reproductions of the original 3 stills bought second-hand by William Grant in 1886. They were directly heated by coal fires until 2004, when they were changed to gas heating. Glenfiddich's pale golden colour and delicate flavour derive from the use of lightly peated malt and maturation principally in American ex-bourbon oak casks. However, the distillery has also been producing some spirit from heavily-peated malt since 2002, which we look forward to tasting with great interest.

Glenfiddich Special Reserve 12 years old (profiled) is the world's best-selling single malt whisky, available in over 200 countries. Glenfiddich Caoran Reserve 12 years old is a peatier version, having been finished in Islay casks. Glenfiddich Solera Reserve is an unusual single malt crafted from whiskies matured in American bourbon, oloroso sherry and new oak casks. The whiskies from all three types of cask are then married in a large Solera European oak vat. Because it is always at least half full, the reservoir of older whiskies in the Solera vat continue to mature. The newer whiskies thus combine with older ones and the resulting malt is drawn off into marrying tuns for a further six month's maturation. Glenfiddich Solera Reserve is a delightfully complex, multi-dimensional single malt whisky at least 15 years old, with vanilla, fruit, cream and sherry highlights. *Whisky Analyst* classified it into Cluster A.

Glenfiddich single malts are also available as Ancient Reserve 18 years old, Gran Reserva 21 years old, Vintage Reserve 1972, and at 30, 40 and 50 years old. There is also a Glenfiddich 1991 version, dedicated to head cooper Dom Ramsay, and a Glenfiddich Malt Whisky Liqueur. Visitors to the distillery can fill, seal and date their own bottle of Glenfiddich Distillery cask-strength malt whisky.

The distillery has an excellent visitor centre offering an audio-visual film in

six languages, guided tours, whisky tastings in the Brand Centre, and a well-stocked shop. It also has a cafeteria providing light snacks, beverages and a licensed bar. It is the only Highland distillery at which visitors can view the whole production process, from mashing the barley malt to bottling the whisky. It is open all year and is definitely worth a visit. Whisky enthusiasts should plan ahead and book the Connoisseurs Tour, with a tutored nosing and tasting of several malts. Further details are at *glenfiddich.com*.

Feature	Profile
●	Body
●●●	Sweetness
●	Smoky
	Medicinal
	Tobacco
	Honey
	Spicy
	Winey
	Nutty
●●	Malty
●●	Fruity
●●	Floral

Age 12 years
Strength 40%
Nose Light, fresh and fragrant with a touch of pine
Taste Medium-sweet with a delicate harmony of malty, citric and floral flavours and a hint of peat
Cluster G Medium-bodied, sweet, low peat and floral notes
Similar to Dufftown, Glen Spey, Speyburn

GLEN GARIOCH

{*glen*-GEAR-*ee*}

Glen Garioch distillery is one of the oldest in Scotland. It is named after the valley of the Garioch, the Granary of Aberdeenshire, where the finest Scottish barley is grown. It definitely existed in 1798 under Thomas Simpson, but other records suggest it was operating in 1785. It was extended to 3 stills in 1973 and has suffered several periods of closure, most recently in the mid 1990s. Happily, this charming distillery in the Aberdeenshire village of Old Meldrum was refurbished by the present owners and reopened in 1997. It boasts some fine Victorian granite buildings with traditional floor maltings, topped by twin pagoda chimneys. The emblem on the bottle is a highland stag, wild herds of which roam around the six summits of nearby Bennochie mountain.

The process water is drawn from springs on Percock Hill, on the estate of Meldrum House. Until 1997 the distillery operated its own floor maltings with peat cut locally from Pitsligo Moss. The present malt is, therefore fairly heavily peated, but they should be much less peaty in future editions, as malted barley is now supplied un-peated to order.

The distillery operates a stainless steel mash tun, 8 stainless steel washbacks, 1 wash still and 2 smaller spirit stills. The whisky is matured in ex-bourbon American oak and ex-sherry European oak casks, in warehouses at the site.

In addition to Glen Garioch Single Highland Malt whisky at 12 years old (profiled) it is also available at 10,15 and 21 years old and in special single cask editions such as a rare 1958 vintage at 46 years old. The whiskies have won several awards in international competitions, especially the 21 years old,

Feature	Profile
●●	Body
●	Sweetness
●●●	Smoky
	Medicinal
	Tobacco
	Honey
●●●	Spicy
●	Winey
	Nutty
●●	Malty
●●	Fruity
●●	Floral

Age 12 years
Strength 43%
Nose Heather fire smoke, together with lavender and a whiff of sherry
Taste Complex oak and raisin notes, canned peaches and cream, with malty and cinnamon notes
Cluster H Medium-bodied, medium-sweet, with smoky, fruity, spicy notes and floral, nutty hints
Similar to Teaninich, Balblair, Glenmorangie

which has won two gold medals.

Glen Garioch distillery has a new visitor centre and offers tours and tastings. It also hosts special events, such as Offshore Europe, a biennial festival for the oil industry.

GLENGOYNE

{*glen*-GOY'*n*}

Burnfoot distillery probably operated illegally in the early part of the nineteenth century, gaining its first licence to distil whisky in 1833. It was renamed "Glen Guin", or "the valley of the wild geese", when Lang Brothers bought it in 1876. While there has been some modernisation over the years, it retains a nineteenth-century charm. It nestles prettily in a wooded valley below Dumgoyne hill, from which the Glengoyne Burn courses through sandstone and over a spectacular 15 metre (49 feet) waterfall, eventually flowing into Loch Lomond.

Glengoyne distillery draws its soft process water from Loch Carron and its cooling water from the Glengoyne Burn. It uses only Scottish barley, Golden Promise and Chariot varieties, air dried after germination and hence unpeated. The carton boldly states "Scotland's Unpeated Malt", which is the whisky's signature. The distillery operates a medium-sized copper domed mash tun, 6 Oregon pine washbacks, 1 wash still and 2 smaller spirit stills with boil balls in the necks and level lyne arms. The size and shape of the spirit stills and boil balls contribute greatly through catalysis and reflux to the flavour of the resulting spirit. The whisky is matured in a combination of refill and sherry casks, in dunnage warehouses at the site.

Glengoyne Single Highland Malt whisky is available at 10 years old (profiled) and at 17, 21 and 30 years old. There are special editions, such as Glengoyne 12 years old cask strength, a Spring 1972 vintage, a 31 years old single cask, and a 28 years old vintage mounted in a miniature brass spirit safe. A rare Glengoyne Scottish oak edition was aged 15 years in a sherry butt and

finished in a cask made of Scottish Oak. The whisky is used in blends such as Cutty Sark, Famous Grouse and Lang's Supreme.

Glengoyne's heritage centre is a converted nineteenth-century warehouse. It is open all year and offers an audio-visual film about the history of the distillery, guided tours, tastings and a shop. It is also possible to start a tour in summer with a dram at the waterfall, and there are also evening events such as blending competitions and corporate hospitality.

Feature	Profile
●	Body
●●	Sweetness
	Smoky
	Medicinal
	Tobacco
●	Honey
●	Spicy
●	Winey
●●	Nutty
●●	Malty
●●●	Fruity
●●	Floral

Age 10 years
Strength 40%
Nose Rich malty aroma with honeysuckle and sherry
Taste Oak, apple and butter notes, hints of sherry and spice, and a long fruity finish
Cluster D Light, medium-sweet, low or no peat, with fruity, floral, malty notes and nutty hints
Similar to Auchentoshan, Glentauchers, Arran

GLEN GRANT

{*glen*-GRANT}

len Grant distillery was founded in 1840 by brothers John and James Grant, who were among the first to be licensed in the Scottish Highlands. The distillery's most famous owner was James Grant's son, Major James Grant, who travelled extensively in India and southern Africa at the end of the nineteenth century. Major Grant's Victorian garden boasts a fine collection of woodland plants, mature orchards, a lily pond and rare exotic plants from around the world. Although the distillery has been substantially extended, many of the original buildings remain, clustered around the Grants' nineteenth-century house with its turrets, gables and courtyard – a fine example of the old Scottish Baronial style.

The distillery's water is drawn from the Caperdonich Spring, supplemented by the Back Burn. Its malted barley is supplied unpeated from specialist maltsters, and the distillery operates a stainless steel mash tun, 10 Oregon pine washbacks, 4 wash stills and 4 spirit stills. Fermentation takes 48 hours, using only distillers' yeast. The bulbous stills incorporate an unusual boil ball in the neck and purifiers before the condensers to partially cool the vapours and thus remove the heavier volatiles. The purifier was invented by John Grant in around 1850 and, together with the tall swan-necked stills, has the effect of producing a very light, delicate spirit.

The stills were directly heated by coal fires until 1996, and rummagers were used to remove burnt solids and burnish the interiors, thereby increasing the exposure of the low wines to copper and enhancing the flavour of the spirit. The present 10 years old malt was produced before the distillery converted to steam heating in 1996, and it will be interesting to see whether this significantly changes the flavour of the whisky.

Glen Grant malt whiskies are well known throughout the world, being among the first to be sold internationally as single malts. The bulk of Glen Grant's production of 6 million litres a year is sold in Italy, where it is the market leader; although it carries no age statement, it is matured in American ex-bourbon oak casks for

5 years. The profiled malt is Glen Grant 10 years old, matured in a mixture of bourbon and sherry casks. Glen Grant is also available at 25 and 30 years old, and at 14 years old cask-strength non chill-filtered. Several Glen Grant vintages are bottled by Gordon & MacPhail, ranging from a rare 1949 to a recent 1989.

The visitor centre includes an exhibition with a short film and there is also a shop. Visitors can sample Glen Grant's two malt whiskies in Major Grant's Study (below left) or in the Dram Hut near the top of the garden (opposite), if the weather is fine.

Feature	Profile
●	Body
●●	Sweetness
	Smoky
	Medicinal
	Tobacco
●	Honey
	Spicy
●	Winey
●●	Nutty
●	Malty
●●	Fruity
●	Floral

Age 10 years
Strength 40%
Nose Light, fragrant, slightly honeyed and floral with a hint of sherry
Taste Clean, slightly sweet with a nutty, fruity flavour reminiscent of apples and pears
Cluster D Light, medium-sweet, low or no peat, with fruity, floral, malty notes and nutty hints
Similar to Glengoyne, Speyside, Aultmore

GLEN KEITH

{*glen*-KEITH}

The attractive buildings at Glen Keith distillery were constructed from a former meal mill using local schist stone.

Glen Keith distillery was built in 1959 beside the Linn of Keith, a beautiful waterfall at the foot of the ruins of Milton Castle. It is a most attractive distillery, rebuilt from a former mill using local stone. The waterfall feeds into a deep pool in the River Isla, where wild salmon leap and swim, hence the emblem on the label depicts a salmon leaping above the Linn pool.

It draws its water from springs on Balloch Hill, and uses lightly peated malted barley. Originally designed for triple distillation with 3 stills, it was converted to double distillation in 1970 and extended to 6 stills working in pairs. The first gas-fired stills were installed here in 1957 and it pioneered the use of computers to control the whole production process, from milling to distillation. The whisky is matured in American borbon hogsheads and some European oak refill sherry casks.

Glen Keith Single Highland Malt whisky is available at 10 years old (profiled), in Gordon & MacPhail's Connoisseurs Choice range 1993 vintage, and from Duncan Taylor. It is also used in blends such as Chivas Regal, 100 Pipers and Scottish Passport.

It does not have a visitor centre.

Feature	Profile
●●	Body
●●●	Sweetness
●	Smoky
	Medicinal
	Tobacco
●	Honey
●●	Spicy
●	Winey
●●	Nutty
●	Malty
●●	Fruity
●	Floral

Age 10 years
Strength 43%
Nose Fragrant, apples and bananas, vanilla and chocolate
Taste Medium-sweet, fruity, dried dates, figs and almonds, and hints of cedar wood and sherry
Cluster F Medium-bodied, medium-sweet, low peat, malty notes and sherry, honey, spicy hints
Similar to Auchroisk, Tullibardine, Glenrothes

PRODUCE OF SCOTLAND

GLENKEITH

SINGLE HIGHLAND MALT
SCOTCH WHISKY

AGED **10** YEARS

A fragrant whisky from the heart of the Highlands. GLEN KEITH is prized by experts for its purity and depth of flavour.

GLEN KEITH is matured for more than ten years in oak casks. The whisky is then bottled under the supervision of our Head Distiller.

The pool of the Salmon

The Glen Keith distillery stands beside the fast-flowing river Isla, above a deep pool where wild salmon swim and leap. The Gaelic name is 'linne a bhradan'. Here, nature is unspoilt; the air and the water pure and sweet. It is in the very heart of Scotch Whisky country.

70 cl ℮

BOTTLED IN SCOTLAND

43%vol

GLENKINCHIE

{glen-KIN-chee}

Established in 1837 by farmers John and George Rate, Glenkinchie Distillery was rebuilt in the 1890s, and is a fine example of a Victorian distillery incorporating listed maltings. Its name "Kinchie" is derived from the "de Quincey" family who originally owned the land and burn.

The distillery lies to the south-east of Edinburgh, in the picturesque "Garden of Scotland", perfect for growing barley and described by Robert Burns as "the most glorious corn country I have ever seen". The eighteenth-century Agricultural Revolution brought barley to East Lothian, often grown on land that had been enriched with local seaweed from the Firth of Forth. The barley ripened early and was prized for its lightness. The draff from the distillery was used to feed the Glenkinchie beef herd, which won national fatstock championships in the 1950s. There have been numerous sightings of the distillery ghost, always of the same appearance – white hair, long whiskers, white shirt and trousers

tied with string at the ankles. It is thought that he may have been a maltster, as a body was actually found behind the maltings in 1902. Glenkinchie is one of only three working distilleries officially classified as Lowland. Its unusually hard water is drawn through limestone from the Lammermuir Hills and rises in a well beneath one of the warehouses. In 1981 the still house was rebuilt and converted to steam heating. It uses lightly peated malt and has 6 traditional Oregon pine washbacks. The copper wash still is the largest in the industry, distilling 31,000 litres per cycle. A copper worm condenser in a tall cast-iron worm tub is used in preference to the more modern condensers, helping to produce a whisky of great character and depth, which has long been prized by blenders. The whisky is matured in ex-bourbon American oak casks.

Described as "The Edinburgh Malt", Glenkinchie Lowland Scotch whisky is available at 10 years old (profiled) in Diageo's Classic Malts range. It is also available in limited editions, such as a

Feature	Profile
●	Body
●●	Sweetness
●	Smoky
	Medicinal
	Tobacco
●	Honey
●●	Spicy
	Winey
	Nutty
●●	Malty
●●	Fruity
●●	Floral

Age 10 years
Strength 43%
Nose Light, sweet with barley-malt, green grass and a curl of smoke
Taste Fresh and slightly sweet, autumn fruits, harvest flavours and cinnamon, with hints of honey and peat
Cluster E Light, medium-sweet, low peat, with floral, malty notes and fruity, spicy, honey hints
Similar to Glenlossie, Caperdonich, Glenallachie

Distillers Edition 1990 finished in Amontillado sherry butts and a vintage 1987 from Signatory.

The visitor centre is open all year and offers tours and tastings. It includes an exhibition, museum and model distillery built in 1924 for the Empire Exhibition by Basset-Lowke, famed for his model steam engines. The old maltings is now the Museum of Malt Whisky Production, with a wonderful collection of whisky-making artefacts.

GLENLIVET

{*glen*-LIVV-*itt*}

Glenlivet distillery was founded by George Smith, a crofter who had been distilling whisky at his farm at Upper Drumin. When George IV visited Edinburgh in 1822, Sir Walter Scott welcomed him with contraband Glenlivet whisky. The king declared it to be his favourite, to be used thereafter in all the royal toasts. Following the 1823 Act of Parliament to legalise large-scale distilling, Smith obtained the first distillery licence in 1824. This was greatly resented by the glen's illicit whisky-makers, who threatened to burn down Smith's farm and murder him for his treachery. During these early, turbulent years he always carried pistols for defence and mounted a round the clock guard at the distillery.

As his whisky gained fame it became necessary to expand and, in 1859, Smith built the present distillery with his son John Gordon Smith, near the confluence of the rivers Livet and Avon, tributaries of the Spey. "The Glenlivet" was registered as a trademark in 1875 and is now widely recognised throughout the world. Glenlivet uses unpeated malted barley and its cold, soft water is drawn from Josie's Well above the distillery. It operates a stainless steel Lauter mash tun, 8 Oregon pine washbacks and 8 large stills. A proportion of sherry casks are used for maturation, but sherry does not dominate the final malt. Glenlivet Single Malt 12 years old (profiled) is currently America's best-seller. It is also available with an American oak finish, a French Limousin oak reserve at 15 years old, at 16 years old cask strength non chill-filtered and at 18 and 21 years old as "The Glenlivet Archive". Several vintages are available in the Cellar Collection, including a 1967 vintage and an exclusive American Oak finish aged 30 years. It is also used in Chivas Regal, Royal Salute and other blends. Visit *theglenlivet.com* for the latest news.

Glenlivet's visitor centre occupies the former maltings, built in 1859. It is open all year and includes an

exhibition of old tools used in malting, peat cutting, distilling and cooperage and George Smith's original hair-trigger pistols.

Visitors can watch an audio-visual presentation, take a guided tour of the distillery and taste the whiskies in George Smith's study. There is also a small restaurant, and accommodation is available in Minmore house, the original nineteenth-century home of George Smith and his family.

Feature	Profile
●●	Body
●●●	Sweetness
●	Smoky
	Medicinal
	Tobacco
●●	Honey
●●	Spicy
●●	Winey
●	Nutty
●●	Malty
●●	Fruity
●●●	Floral

Age 12 years
Strength 40%
Nose Summer flowers, tart apples, honey, a spicy note and a whiff of smoke
Taste Medium-bodied, perfect balance of rish sweetness, fragrance and fruit, with vanilla and a hint of sherry
Cluster C Medium-bodied, medium-sweet, with fruity, floral, honey, malty notes and spicy hints
Similar to Glen Elgin, Glen Ord, Glendullan

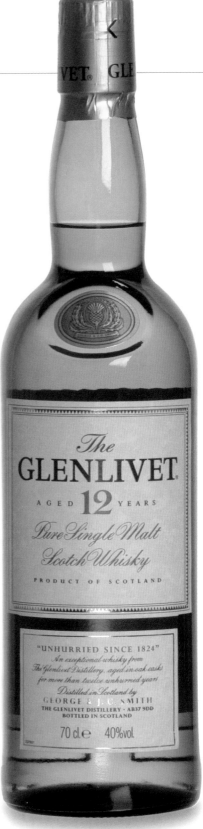

The GLENLIVET
AGED **12** YEARS
Pure Single Malt
Scotch Whisky
PRODUCT OF SCOTLAND

"UNHURRIED SINCE 1824"
An exceptional whisky from The Glenlivet Distillery, aged in oak casks for more than twelve unhurried years. Distilled in Scotland by
GEORGE & J.G. SMITH
THE GLENLIVET DISTILLERY · AB37 9DD
BOTTLED IN SCOTLAND
70 cl e   40%vol.

GLENLOSSIE

{*glen*-LOSSY}

Glenlossie distillery was built in 1876 by John Duff, a publican and former manager of Glendronach distillery. He designed it on a slope to take advantage of gravity and used the 70 foot drop from the large dam to power a water wheel, "thereby rendering it independent of steam power". The distillery was reconstructed in 1896, when a private railway siding was added, and further improvements were made over the years until production ceased in 1917 to conserve barley stocks during World War I. It was again extended in 1962, and converted from coal-fired to steam heating in 1972.

With the exception of the fine stone still house, the buildings were constructed from cement, using sand and gravel from the River Lossie. They have very clean, white lines and classic slate roofs, and there is a single pagoda-topped malt house. A special feature is a fire engine, purpose-built in 1862 and last used when the distillery was badly damaged by fire in 1929.

Glenlossie draws its process water from the Bardon Burn, and cooling water from the Gedloch and Foths Burns. It operates a stainless steel mash tun, 4 stainless steel washbacks and 6 tall stills. Each of the spirit stills has a purifier incorporated between the lyne arm and the condenser to remove the heavier alcohols, thereby producing a lighter spirit.

The label on the bottle features a long-eared owl as its emblem, owing to the presence of owls in the woods nearby.

Glenlossie Single Malt is available at 10 years old (profiled) in Diageo's Flora and Fauna range, and from some independents. It is used in Haig and Dimple blends, which account for the bulk of the production.

Glenlossie Distillery does not have a visitor centre or offer tours.

Feature	Profile
●	Body
●●	Sweetness
●	Smoky
	Medicinal
	Tobacco
●	Honey
●●	Spicy
	Winey
●	Nutty
●●	Malty
●●	Fruity
●●	Floral

Age 10 years
Strength 43%
Nose Light fresh aroma, with grassy, floral notes
Taste Medium-sweet with malt and spice notes, and a hint of smoke
Cluster E Light, medium-sweet, low peat, with floral, malty notes and fruity, spicy, honey hints
Similar to Caperdonich, Glenkinchie, Glenallachie

SPEYSIDE
SINGLE MALT SCOTCH WHISKY

The three *spirit stills* at the

GLENLOSSIE

distillery have *purifiers* installed between the *lyne arm* and the *condenser*. This has a bearing on the *character* of the *single MALT SCOTCH WHISKY* produced which has a *fresh, grassy* aroma and a *smooth*, lingering flavour. Built in 1876 by *John Duff*, the *distillery* lies four miles *south* of ELGIN in *Morayshire*

AGED **10** YEARS

GLENMORANGIE

{glen-MOR-angie}

Glenmorangie is Gaelic for "Glen of Tranquillity". Situated at Tain in the north of Scotland, overlooking the Dornoch Firth, it was founded by William Mathieson in 1849. The adverts emphasize the tranquil setting in which Glenmorangie Single Highland Malt Scotch Whisky is patiently crafted by the distillery's skilled craftsmen, known as the "Sixteen Men of Tain".

The distillery has 8 swan-necked stills, the tallest in Scotland at nearly 17 feet, and it is claimed that these elegant stills produce a lighter, purer spirit. Its water, unusually hard and rich in minerals, is drawn through sandstone from Tarlogie Springs. The whisky is matured in bourbon barrels, made from American oaks at least 100 years old, grown on the north-facing slopes of the

Ozark mountains of Missouri. This slow growth, tight grain white oak minimises the oak effect on the mature whisky, delivering a benchmark malt that retains as much of the original spirit character as possible. To add variety, therefore, Glenmorangie was the first to introduce special wood finishes other than sherry, a trend that has since been widely adopted.

Glenmorangie is available at 10 years old (profiled), at 15, 18 and 30 years old,

and in four special wood finishes – Sherry, Port, Madeira and Burgundy. Other expressions include Artisan Cask 9 Years old, Cellar 13, Traditional, Madeira Matured 1988, Truffle Oak Reserve and Malaga Cask Finish 30 years old. Glenmorangie "Speakeasy" is also available at the distillery, filled directly from the cask.

Glenmorangie distillery is open all year for tours and tastings. Visitors are shown an audio-visual film in a converted still house, with a working steam engine and a model still. Virtual tours are available at *glenmorangie.com*.

Feature	Profile
●●	Body
●●	Sweetness
●	Smoky
●	Medicinal
	Tobacco
●	Honey
●●	Spicy
	Winey
●●	Nutty
●	Malty
●●	Fruity
●●	Floral

Age 10 years
Strength 40%
Nose Flora, vanilla, citrus fruits and butterscotch
Taste Creamy, soft and fresh with fruit, flowers, spice and nuts – the true character of a delicate spirit, unspoiled by strong oak influences
Cluster H Medium-bodied, medium-sweet, with smoky, fruity, spicy notes and floral, nutty hints
Similar to Balblair, Strathmill, Craigellachie

GLEN MORAY

{*glen*-MURRAY}

Glen Moray distillery nestles on the banks of the River Lossie in Elgin, Speyside's ancient royal capital. It opened as a distillery in 1897 on the site of a former brewery beside Gallow Hill, Elgin's former gallows. In 1962 when the distillery grounds were excavated for a new warehouse, seven skulls were uncovered, one of which had a musket ball enbedded in the jaw. Although the last hanging was in 1697, there is still a brooding eeriness to this spot, suitable orchestration being provided by the resident rooks as they circle and dive from their nests in the rustling pines on the hill. The original road into Elgin runs through the distillery and some of Scotland's legendary figures are said to have passed this way. They include St Columba, King Duncan, Macbeth and Bonnie Prince Charlie.

Glen Moray draws its water from a well beside the River Lossie and uses lightly peated malted barley. It operates a stainless steel mash tun, 5 stainless steel washbacks and 4 squat onion-shaped stills. The whisky is mostly matured in ex-bourbon American oak casks, with a few special casks reserved for limited editions, in traditional dunnage warehouses at the site.

Glen Moray Speyside Single Malt Whisky is available at 12 years old (profiled), and at 16, 20 and 30 years old. The flagship expression, Glen Moray Classic, is now the second best-selling malt in Scotland. The Distillery Manager's Choice expressions range from 1962 to 1992 vintages, a 1986 Centenary edition, and others from 1984 to 1989 – visit *glenmoray.com* for the current range.

Glen Moray's visitor centre, open all year for tours and tastings, was recently awarded 4-star status by the Scottish Tourist Board. Guided tours by distillery workers give visitors the opportunity to learn first-hand the secrets of their historic craft. The new café opened in 2004 and the distillery has been invited to join the Malt Whisky Trail.

Feature	Profile
●	Body
●●	Sweetness
●	Smoky
	Medicinal
	Tobacco
●	Honey
●●	Spicy
●	Winey
●●	Nutty
●●	Malty
●●	Fruity
●●●●	Floral

Age 12 years
Strength 40%
Nose Fruity and creamy with vanilla, citrus and heather notes
Taste Nutty and spicy, with fruit, floral and menthol flavours and a whiff of smoke
Cluster E Light, medium-sweet, low peat, with floral, malty notes and fruity, spicy, honey hints
Similar to Caperdonich, Bunnahabhain, Glenburgie

GLEN ORD

{*glen*-ORD}

Just north of Inverness, on Eilean Dubh – the legendary "Black Isle" – can be found Glen Ord Distillery. It was first licensed for whisky production in 1838 by Robert Johnstone and Donald McLennan, but records of an alehouse and meal mill date from 1549. Indeed it was John Mackenzie's sixteenth-century meal mill that provided the focus of village life at Muir of Ord for 4 centuries, where local farmers would bring their oats and barley to be milled. The modernised Ord Maltings now supplies malted barley to several other distilleries in north-west Scotland, using a combination of local peat and oil-fired kilns.

Glen Ord Distillery was extensively modified and refurbished in 1896, when it ranked as one of the top distilleries in Scotland with a workforce of around 100 men. Sturdy Clydesdale horses and carts transported milled meal and whisky to the railway station at Muir of Ord, returning with fresh barley for the maltings – it was not unknown for the carter to be "the worse o' wear", relying on his horse to find its way back to the maltings. The distillery was lit by paraffin lamps until 1939, when electricity was first connected.

Glen Ord is the last of 9 distilleries that operated around Muir of Ord in the nineteenth century. The rich agricultural land of the Black Isle produces fine barley, and offers an ideal location for whisky production with its plentiful supply of peat and continuous pure peaty water flowing from Loch nan Eun and Loch nan Bonnach into Allt Fionnaidh (the "white burn"). Peat is traditionally cut from Drumossie Moor, the site of the battle of Culloden, so the spirit may be infused with Highland blood.

Until recently, Glen Ord whisky was mostly used for blending; but Glen Ord Hidden Malt 12 years old (profiled) was re-launched in the 1990s with immediate success, winning several international awards. Not that exporting is a new venture at Glen Ord – in its nineteenth-century heyday, Alfred Barnard recorded that the whisky was shipped to "Singapore, South Africa and other colonies". Glen Ord 1975 Vintage Malt is also available in the Rare Malts range.

The distillery's visitor centre, a converted warehouse, is open all year, offering tours and tastings. It includes an attractive exhibition on the history of the distillery and the Black Isle. Visitors can purchase a range of whiskies and other goods in the distillery shop.

Feature	Profile
●●●	Body
●●	Sweetness
●	Smoky
	Medicinal
	Tobacco
●	Honey
●●	Spicy
●	Winey
●	Nutty
●●	Malty
●●	Fruity
●●	Floral

Age 12 years
Strength 40%
Nose Malty, sweet with hints of sherry and smoke
Taste Medium-bodied, spicy fruit and floral flavour, with barley-sugar and sherry notes and a long malty finish
Cluster C Medium-bodied, medium-sweet, with fruity, floral, honey, malty notes and spicy hints
Similar to Glendullan, Glenlivet, BenRiach

GLENROTHES

{*glen*-ROTH-*is*}

The Glen of Dounie at the fringe of Rothes is the pretty location for Glenrothes distillery, which lies on the banks of the peaty burn of Rothes and is flanked by the ancient village graveyard. The distillery draws its water from Ardcanny Spring, known locally as "The Lady's Well" after the only daughter of the fourteenth-century Earl of Rothes. Legend has it that she was murdered beside the spring by the "Wolf of Badenoch" while trying to protect her lover.

Fine malt whisky has been distilled here since Glenrothes first opened in 1879. The distillery was extended in 1896, but a fire on 15th May 1922 caused many casks to explode and large quantities of matured whisky poured into the burn. It is said that the locals enjoyed a free toddy from the burn that day, scooping it up in pots, pans and even their boots. An angler claimed that the trout, unusually docile from the whisky in the water, were easily caught!

Glenrothes Distillery was fully modernised in 1980 and produces 1.6 million litres per annum. It operates a large, stainless steel mash tun producing 4 tonnes of mash per cycle, 12 Oregon pine washbacks, 5 low wines stills and 5 spirit stills. Fermentation lasts about two days, and only cultured yeast is used. The spirit stills are unusually larger and have a higher charge than the wash stills, resulting in less copper catalysis and a lighter, delicate spirit. The whole process, including distillation, is controlled automatically from the still room by a sophisticated computer system. The lightly peated malt used at the distillery is supplied to order from Tamdhu Maltings, and the whisky is matured in a mixture of Spanish and American oak casks, prepared with both sherry and bourbon.

Limited quantities of the best casks are individually selected from a given year's distillation, when judged to be at the peak of their perfection, and bottled as the Glenrothes Vintage Malt for that year. Not all the casks from one year necessarily meet the Master Blender's high quality criteria and, therefore, a "vintage" is not produced every year. Each bottle carries the date of distillation and year of bottling – the profiled malt was distilled in 1989, bottled in 2000, and hence matured for 11 years.

Glenrothes is sold in a clear glass bottle that reflects the style of sample bottles typically found in a blending room. This understated bottle emphasises the quality of the whisky, which is highly prized by many Master Blenders. The bulk of the production goes for blending, and Glenrothes is the signature malt in Cutty Sark Scots Whisky, a premium blend sold worldwide by Cutty Sark International. Glenrothes is also available from Gordon & MacPhail at 8 years old (the MacPhail's Collection) and separately as a vintage. Glenrothes distillery is not open to the public.

Feature	Profile
●●	Body
●●●	Sweetness
●	Smoky
	Medicinal
	Tobacco
●	Honey
●	Spicy
●●	Winey
●	Nutty
●●	Malty
●●	Fruity
	Floral

Age 12 years
Strength 43%
Nose Rich, sweet and honeyed, with sherry, vanilla and malt evident
Taste Medium-smooth body, light smoke, multi-layered with hints of fruit, vanilla and spice, and a long finish
Cluster F Medium-bodied, medium-sweet, low peat, malty notes and sherry, honey, spicy hints
Similar to Auchroisk, Deanston, Glen Keith

GLEN SCOTIA

{*glen*-SCO-*sha*}

In the ancient town of Campbeltown, the Celtic lord Dalruadhain crowned Scotland's early kings on the Stone of Destiny. At the end of the eighteenth century, there were at least 34 illicit stills operating here, and Glen Scotia distillery was probably one of them, although it was not licensed until 1835. By 1887, Campbeltown had 21 licensed distillers, producing 10 million litres of whisky a year and employing over 250 men. In the 1960s it featured in a minor hit record by the singer Andie Stewart, with the memorable line "Oh Campbeltown Loch I wish you were whisky, I would drink you dry".

Campbeltown has long enjoyed a reputation as the "cradle" of Scotch whisky – in 1887, Alfred Barnard described it as "whisky city". It is the only town to have been listed as a whisky region. It was used as a source by bootleggers during American prohibition, but the quality of its whisky declined and most of the producers ceased operating. Sadly, only three distilleries now operate in Campbeltown – Springbank and Glen Scotia.

Glen Scotia operates a small distillery that could easily be mistaken for a Victorian townhouse. It has its own resident ghost, a previous owner Duncan MacCallum who drowned himself in Campbeltown Loch and returns to haunt the night shift. The distillery was reconstructed in 1894 and substantially upgraded in 1992. Following a further period of silence, it resumed production in 1999.

Its water is drawn from two deep wells below the distillery and from Crosshill Loch and it uses moderately peated malted barley. It operates a steel mash tun, 6 steel wash backs and 2 swan-necked stills. The whisky is matured in a mixture of American bourbon oak, European sherry casks, and some refills racked 9 high in a modern warehouse at the distillery.

Glen Scotia Single Malt whisky is available at 14 years old (profiled), and

at 8 years old. It is quite typical of the briny, peaty malt whiskies formerly produced in Campbeltown. We look forward to the new whiskies becoming available at the end of the decade.

Glen Scotia® distillery does not have a visitor centre but offers tours in summer, by appointment, and has a small shop.

Feature	Profile
●●	Body
●●	Sweetness
●●	Smoky
●●	Medicinal
	Tobacco
●	Honey
	Spicy
●	Winey
●●	Nutty
●●	Malty
●	Fruity
●	Floral

Age 14 years
Strength 40%
Nose Lightly perfumed, malty and peaty notes, with a salty tang
Taste Medium-bodied, not too sweet, spirity with nutty, honey notes and light fruit
Cluster I Medium-light, dry, with smoky, spicy, honey notes and nutty, floral hints
Similar to Highland Park, Springbank, Isle of Jura

PRODUCT OF SCOTLAND

CAMPBELTOWN
SINGLE
MALT

AGED **12** YEARS

SCOTCH
WHISKY

GLEN SCOTIA DISTILLERY
ARGYLLSHIRE, SCOTLAND

70cl ℮   40%vol

GLEN SCOTIA

SCOTIA DIST

GLEN SPEY

{*glen*-SPEY}

G len Spey distillery was built at Rothes in 1885 by James Stuart, who also owned Macallan until 1892. It was originally an extension to the Mill of Rothes, and retains pleasant Victorian buildings, though it was rebuilt in 1969 when extended to 4 stills. It stands below the ruins of Castle Rothes, the home of the Earls of Rothes since the fourteenth century. Castle Rothes was unfortunately burnt down by locals in 1620 to prevent it becoming a refuge for thieves.

It draws its water from the Doonie Burn and uses lightly peated malted barley. It operates a semi-Lauter mash tun, 8 stainless steel washbacks and 4 stills. In fact, Glen Spey was the first to install this type of mash tun. The whisky is matured in ex-bourbon and refill casks, stored in traditional warehouses at the distillery. The emblem on the label is the Goldcrest, Britain's smallest bird, which can be heard warbling in the Scots pines beside Castle Rothes.

Glen Spey Single Highland Malt whisky is available at 12 years old (profiled), and from some independents. The bulk of the production goes for blending, and it is used principally in Diageo's J&B blend and in Spey Royal.

Glen Spey distillery does not have a visitor centre or offer tours.

Feature	Profile
●	Body
●●●	Sweetness
●	Smoky
	Medicinal
	Tobacco
	Honey
●	Spicy
●	Winey
●	Nutty
●●	Malty
	Fruity
●●	Floral

Age 12 years
Strength 40%
Nose Aromatic, malty and floral with a peppered tang
Taste Light and sweet, with a malty, grassy character, roast chestnuts and hints of smoke and spice
Cluster G Medium-bodied, sweet, low peat and floral notes
Similar to Glenfiddich, Miltonduff, Dufftown

SPEYSIDE
SINGLE MALT
SCOTCH WHISKY

The Scots Pines beside *the ruins of ROTHES CASTLE,* provide an *ideal habitat* for the *GOLDCREST, Britain's smallest bird,* and overlook the

GLEN SPEY

distillery. Founded in 1885, *the distillery was originally* part of the *Mills of Rothes.* Water *from the DOONIE BURN* is used to produce this *smooth, warming single MALT SCOTCH WHISKY.* A slight sense of *wood smoke on the nose* is rewarded with a *spicy, dry* finish.

A G E D 12 Y E A R S

45% vol   Distilled & Bottled in SCOTLAND   70cl
GLEN SPEY DISTILLERY Rothes, Aberlour, Banffshire, Scotland

GLENTAUCHERS

{ben-RIN-is}

Glentauchers distillery was founded in 1897 at Tauchers Farm near Mulben by blenders William Lowrie and James Buchanan, expressly to supply malt whisky for blending, which resulted in Buchanan formulating his famous "Black and White" blend. The location was chosen for its proximity to the Great Highland railway line, and for the supply of clear soft water flowing from the Hill of Towie into the River Isla. At Packhorse Bridge nearby there is a deep pool, Guan's Pot, where witches were thrown to test whether they were in league with the devil. If Auld Nick supported them and they floated, they were burnt. If they were innocent, then they sank and drowned.

The distillery was designed by local Keith architect John Alcock, and built by the famous firm of Charles Doig & Son of Elgin. It took twelve months to complete and started working in May 1898. Its water, collected from Rosarie Burn by a dam above the distillery, powered everything by turbine until a steam engine was installed in 1955, and it had its own railway siding for the transportation of goods and supplies.

At the turn of the 19th century, Glentauchers was highly advanced for its day. In 1925 it was extensively remodelled by Charles Doig; and in 1966 it was extended to its present layout with a modern still house, mash house and tun room. Most of its original gaunt Victorian buildings have been retained, including a large malt barn with twin pagoda chimneys (pictured), and the excise officer's and chief brewer's houses.

Floor malting ceased in 1969, and its malted barley is now supplied un-peated to order. It operates a traditional copper-domed cast iron mash tun, 6 larch washbacks and 6 conventional pot stills. The whisky is mostly matured in American bourbon hogsheads. More recently, Glentauchers distillery pioneered an automated system for spray cleaning the heating elements to remove burnt yeast residues.

Glentauchers Single Malt Scotch Whisky is available at 15 years old 46% (profiled) in the Allied Distilleries Series, and in Gordon & MacPhail's Speyside Malt range as a 1990 vintage. It is used in Ballantines and Teachers blends.

Feature	Profile
●	Body
●●	Sweetness
	Smoky
	Medicinal
	Tobacco
●	Honey
●	Spicy
	Winey
●●	Nutty
●●	Malty
●●●	Fruity
●●●	Floral

Age 15 years
Strength 46%
Nose Fragrant and sweet with cooking apples, sugared almonds and leafy orchards
Taste Light bodied aperitif, fruity and floral, with summer fruits and a short finish
Cluster D Light, medium-sweet, low or no peat, with fruity, floral, malty notes and nutty hints
Similar to Auchentoshan, Glengoyne, Cardhu

GLENTURRET

{*glen*-TURRET}

Built in 1775 and licensed in 1826, Glenturret is Scotland's oldest working distillery. Despite being one of the smallest distilleries in Scotland, it is also the most visited, offering fine hospitality to 200,000 visitors a year. The reasons for its popularity include its central location an hour's drive from Glasgow and Edinburgh, its picturesque setting and its excellent facilities as the home of "The Famous Grouse".

Nestling beside the Turret Burn, near Crieff in Perthshire, Glenturret is a traditional farm distillery, distilling its whiskies in relatively small quantities using squat pot stills. Its most famous resident was Towser, whose 24 years of duty as distillery cat are commemorated by a bronze statue and an entry in the Guinness Book of Records. Look out for Towser's

successors, the present distillery cat team of Dylan and Brooke.

Glenturret Single Highland Malt is available at 10 years old (profiled), and in limited editions such as 1972 and 1987 vintages hand-signed by the distillery manager. Glenturret whiskies are well balanced and have won many awards.

Visitors are welcome at Glenturret Distillery all year round. The Famous Grouse Experience presents the "Flight of the Grouse", a BAFTA Award-winning interactive show, and a "Spirit of the Glen" exhibition. As well as a guided tour, there is a chance to sample Glenturret, Macallan and Highland Park single malts, and a range of award-winning Famous Grouse blended malt whiskies in the Nosing and Tasting Bar. The extensive catering facilities include the Famous Restaurant, a converted warehouse where visitors can enjoy anything from morning coffee to a three-course meal. There is also the Famous gift shop and a conference suite, with modern audio-visual facilities and flexible lecture accommodation. Evening functions, such as Burns' night suppers and *ceilidhs*, are also available, for which advance booking is essential.

Feature	Profile
●●	Body
●●●	Sweetness
●	Smoky
	Medicinal
	Tobacco
●●	Honey
●●	Spicy
●●	Winey
●●	Nutty
●●	Malty
●	Fruity
●●	Floral

Age 10 years
Strength 40%
Nose Floral, malty and peppery, with a whiff of smoke
Taste Light, medium-sweet, well-balanced with nutty, malty notes and hints of honey, vanilla and spices
Cluster B Medium-bodied, medium-sweet, with nutty, malty, floral, honey and fruity notes
Similar to Knockando, Aberfeldy, Blair Athol

HIGHLAND PARK

{*high-land*-PARK}

Situated on the island of Orkney to the west of Kirkwall, Highland Park is the most northerly distillery in the world. It was founded by Magnus Eunson in the late 18th century, one of many Orcadian smugglers and illicit whisky producers who rebelled against the heavy excise duties imposed to finance the war with Napoleon. It is said that he used his position as church officer to conceal whisky beneath the church pulpit. The distillery was licensed in 1826 by Robert Borwick, whose son-in-law, the local Exciseman John Robertson, is generally credited with routing out the smugglers. It was

no coincidence that Robertson had acquired the distillery and surrounding land from Magnus Eunson prior to Borwick commencing legal production.

Highland Park is one of the few distilleries to use hard water, and its supply is drawn from Cattie Maggie's Springs. Also unusual is the use of traditional floor maltings for germinating the barley, which is then dried over a fire of local aromatic heather peat, cut from nearby Hobbister Moor. This is the source of the heathery smokiness that is characteristic of Highland Park whiskies, now lightened by adding some unpeated mainland malted barley.

In addition to Highland Park 12 years old (profiled), it is also available at 18, 25 and 30 years old and in special vintages and editions such as Highland Park "Capella", which commemorated the 60th anniversary of Orkney's world-famous Italian Chapel. The whisky is matured mostly in European oak ex-sherry casks with some American ex-bourbon casks for balance. The result is a medium-bodied, multi-layered,

complex malt whisky with peat smoke evident, but by no means dominant, and heather, honey and malty notes.

Highland Park's visitor centre and shop are open on weekdays all year, and also at weekends during the summer. The tour includes an audio-visual presentation about the history of the distillery and its production methods and visitors have the opportunity to taste the whiskies. Sensitive visitors might even meet the ghost of Magnus Eunson on the stairs below the boardroom. If you can't make the trip to Orkney, visit *highlandpark.co.uk.*

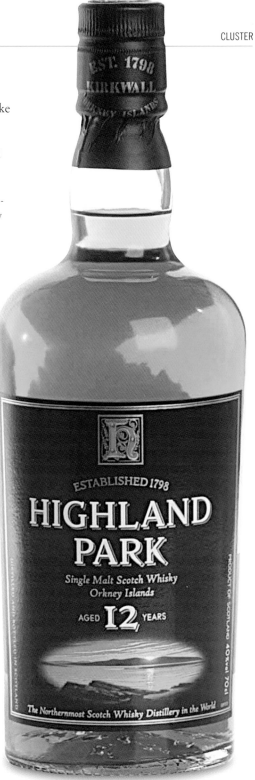

Feature	Profile
●●	Body
●●	Sweetness
●●●	Smoky
●	Medicinal
	Tobacco
●●	Honey
●	Spicy
●	Winey
●	Nutty
●●	Malty
●	Fruity
●	Floral

Age 12 years
Strength 40%
Nose Heather-honey sweetness and peaty smokiness
Taste Medium-bodied, sweet and smoky with layers of mint toffee, heather, malt and honey and a pinch of cumin seeds – delicious
Cluster I Medium-light, dry, with smoky, spicy, honey notes and nutty, floral hints
Similar to Bowmore, Springbank, Bruichladdich

INCHGOWER

{inch-GOW-er}

Inchgower distillery lies on the site of the former Tochieneal distillery, near the village of Rathven and five miles from Fochabers and Buckie. It was established in 1822 by Alexander Wilson on the estate of the Earl of Seafield, being re-named Inchgower when it was re-built in 1871 by the founder's great-nephew, also Alexander Wilson. When Alfred Barnard visited it in 1885, he observed that "the buildings are of stone and slate, erected in the form of an oblong quadrangle... a modern work, fitted with all the latest improvements of machinery and vessels". His book includes three line drawings of the distillery, and today's

visitor would instantly recognise these Victorian buildings in the present format, albeit with the addition of modern warehousing (pictured). It is an attractive distillery with a pretty courtyard, formerly flanked by a

carpenter's shop, cooperage, blacksmith and workers' cottages, and has a stone still house and twin pagoda-topped chimneys, all of which were noted by Barnard. Until the early twentieth century, the adjoining farm reared cattle, sheep and pigs on the burnt ale and draff from the distillery, including champion Aberdeen Angus bulls.

The emblem on the bottle is the oyster catcher, and examples of these birds can be seen on the sands beyond Buckie.

Inchgower's process water is drawn from springs in the Menduff hills, and cooling water is supplied by Buckie Burn, although the original source was Letter Burn. It operates a stainless steel mash tun, 6 Oregon pine washbacks and 4 stills. The whisky is matured in ex-bourbon American oak casks in warehouses at the site. In 1885, Barnard noted that the make was available as a single malt as well as in blends, and that the annual output of 62,000 gallons was

Feature	Profile
●	Body
●●●	Sweetness
●	Smoky
●	Medicinal
	Tobacco
●●	Honey
●●	Spicy
	Winey
●	Nutty
●●	Malty
●	Fruity
●●	Floral

Age 14 years
Strength 43%
Nose Aromatic sweetness, malty and honeyed
Taste Fruity, spicy, and oaky notes, with hints of seaside and smoke
Cluster E Light, medium-sweet, low peat, with floral, malty notes and fruity, spicy, honey hints
Similar to Tomintoul, Glenallachie, Glenlossie

usually all sold before it was manufactured. It was highly sought after in England and the colonies.

Inchgower Single Malt is available at 14 years old (profiled) in Diageo's Flora and Fauna range, and at 22 years old in the Rare Malts range. It is now used in Bell's blends, which account for most of its production.

Inchgower does not have a visitor centre or offer tours.

ISLE OF JURA

{*isle-o'*-JEW-*ra*}

It is estimated that the red deer of the Hebridean island of Jura outnumber the human population by thirty to one. Indeed, the name Jura is Norse for "deer island". Nestling at Craighouse, in the shadow of the Paps of Jura which tower 2,575 feet (785 m) above, lies the distillery. The Gulf Stream means the climate is mild and palm trees flourish. To get there, take the Feolin Ferry from Islay and follow the road – there is only one. George Orwell wrote his novel *1984* here, a fact commemorated by an Isle of Jura 1984 edition distilled in that year.

It is claimed that whisky has been distilled here since 1502. The present distillery was established in 1810 and in 1886 Alfred Barnard visited and fell in love with it. He wrote that it was "one of the handsomest we had seen and looks more like a castle than a

distillery". Jura's population was then about 1,000 – today it is less than a quarter of that.

Its water rises from the Bhaile Mhargaidh spring, running over quartzite and heather. Using lightly peated malt, the distillery produces a light, dry whisky that is not typical of other island malts, and provides Jura's only industry after farming and fishing. After a period of closure (1918–60), it was rebuilt in 1960 and extended in the 1970s to 4 large stills that are more like a Highland distillery than those of its neighbours on Islay.

Isle of Jura Single malt is available at 10 years old (profiled), at 16, 21 and 36 years old. It is also available as Isle of Jura Legacy 10 years old from sherry casks, a 13 year old cask-strength edition and a 30 year old single

Feature	Profile
●●	Body
●	Sweetness
●●	Smoky
●●	Medicinal
	Tobacco
●	Honey
●	Spicy
	Winey
●●	Nutty
●	Malty
●	Fruity
●	Floral

Age 10 years
Strength 40%
Nose Aromatic and dry, orange zest and almond, a whiff of smoke and salt spray
Taste Light and dry, with fruit and peaty notes and the suggestion of heather, almonds and pine
Cluster I Medium-light, dry, with smoky, spicy, honey notes and nutty, floral hints
Similar to Bruichladdich, Springbank, Glen Scotia

cask bottling. There is an un-aged Isle of Jura Superstition, which combines heavily peated younger malt with older Jura to deliver a subtle Islay style. It won a gold medal at the International Wine and Spirit Competition in 2004.

The distillery has a visitor centre, and tours can be arranged by appointment, or visit *isleofjura.com* for more information.

KNOCKANDO

{*knock*-AN-*do*}

Knockando, in Gaelic "Cnoc-an-dhu", means the "little black hill". Bonnie Prince Charlie's army camped here on the banks of the Spey in 1745, on their way to the fateful battle of Culloden. The distillery was built in 1898 by J Thompson, a spirit broker of Elgin. The site was chosen for its plentiful supply of clear water from the Cardnach Spring and its proximity to the Great North of Scotland railway line. It is claimed that the special purity of this water determines the unique character of Knockando malt whiskies. The distillery sits on a steeply wooded bank of the River Spey, and its pagoda chimney and whitewashed walls rise majestically from the surrounding dense forest. It was extended in 1969 with the addition of two stills and a new stillhouse, but several buildings retain a Victorian charm, including a former station that is now used as a trade centre (pictured).

Knockando is the heart of J&B blended whisky, one of the world's best-selling blends. When Prime Minister Margaret Thatcher presented the company with the Queen's Award for Export Achievement here in 1985, she received the billionth bottle of J&B Rare ever to be produced.

The water is drawn from the Cardnach Spring, and it uses very lightly peated barley. The distillery operates a stainless steel mash tun, 8 Oregon pine washbacks and 4 pot stills. The bulk of the whisky is matured in ex-bourbon hogsheads for blending, but a few European ex-sherry casks are also used for the malt whisky, imparting a subtle sherry influence and body.

Knockando Speyside Single Malt whisky is available at 12 years old (profiled) and at various vintages, for example Knockando 1992 aged 12 years, Knockando 1980 aged

Feature	Profile
●●	Body
●●●	Sweetness
●	Smoky
	Medicinal
	Tobacco
●●	Honey
●●	Spicy
●	Winey
●●	Nutty
●	Malty
●●	Fruity
●●	Floral

Age 12 years
Strength 40%
Nose Floral, sweet and honeyed, reminiscent of wet gardens in summer
Taste Medium-bodied, subtle flavour with grass, nuts and spice showing, and hints of sherry and smoke
Cluster B Medium-bodied, medium-sweet, with nutty, malty, floral, honey and fruity notes
Similar to Glenturret, Benromach, Scapa

18 years, Knockando 1977 Extra Old, and Knockando Single Cask aged 21 years, and these can be drier. Most of the production goes to the J&B blends, but the Knockando single malt can be obtained through specialist whisky retailers and in export markets.

Knockando does not have a visitor centre, though tours of the distillery are possible by appointment.

LAGAVULIN

*{laga-*VOO*-lin}*

Lagavulin is Gaelic for "the hollow where the mill is". Nestling on the southern coast of Islay, near the brooding ruin of Dunyvaig Castle, it is one of the oldest distilleries in Scotland. In the twelfth century Dunyvaig was occupied by Somerled, the first Lord of the Isles, who is credited with driving the Vikings from the west of Scotland. Hence Lagavulin's distinctive, complex malt is styled "Lord of the Isles – the definitive Islay malt". The distillery's sharp lines and white buildings, with their twin pagoda-topped chimneys, date from Victorian times and contrast starkly against the rugged foreshore and heather-clad hills beyond.

Whisky has been produced here since the early eighteenth century, with 10 stills thought to have been operating in the 1740s. Lagavulin distillery was first licensed in 1816 to John Johnston. In 1867 the distillery was bought by "restless" Peter Mackie, who created the White Horse Scotch blend with Lagavulin at its heart.

The distillery's water is drawn from Solan Lochs, having passed through heavy peat bogs which, together with the heavily peated malted barley, contributes to its distinctively pungent character. The barley is malted to order at Port Ellen Maltings, having been dried over a fire of peat cut from a local moss. The distillery operates a large stainless steel mash tun, 10 larch washbacks, and 4 squat onion-shaped stills with broad necks and steeply-angled lyne-arms (pictured).

The whisky is matured in ex-bourbon American oak casks, combined with a few sherry casks for finishing. The casks are stored in the maturation sheds above the beach – it's no surprise, therefore, that the whisky carries a strong whiff of seaweed and fresh, salty Atlantic air.

Lagavulin single malt whisky was being supplied to England and the colonies as early as 1875, but most went for blending until the 1980s, when it

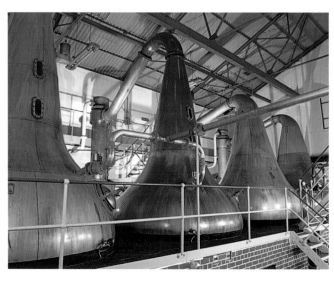

was launched as one of Diageo's Classic Malts. Lagavulin 16 years old (profiled) is now their best seller, with demand far outstripping the supply, and it has won several gold medals in recent international competitions. Lagavulin is also available at 12 years old cask-strength, and in Lagavulin Distillers Editions using sweet Pedro Ximénez sherry casks for the final finish.

Lagavulin distillery has a shop, offers tours and tastings and welcomes visitors on weekdays all year round.

Feature	Profile
●●●●	Body
●	Sweetness
●●●●	Smoky
●●●●	Medicinal
●	Tobacco
	Honey
●	Spicy
●●	Winey
●	Nutty
●	Malty
●	Fruity
	Floral

Age 16 years
Strength 43%
Nose Powerful peat smoke with iodine and seaweed and a hint of malty sweetness
Taste Dry peat smoke, roasted chestnuts and liquorice with a salty, sherried note and a complex finish
Cluster J Full-bodied, dry, pungent, peaty and medicinal, with spicy, tobacco notes
Similar to Laphroaig, Ardbeg, Caol Ila

LAPHROAIG

*{la-*FROY*'g}*

Laphroaig is Gaelic for "the beautiful hollow by the broad bay" and on a sunny day it truly lives up to its name. It was built in 1815 by Donald and Alex Johnston at a remote spot on the windswept southern coast of Islay. Its neat Victorian stone buildings seem almost to challenge the elements – white-washed granite walls with orderly rows of black-framed windows, twin pagoda-topped kilns, warehouses that announce "LAPHROAIG" in tall bold letters that face defiantly across the Atlantic.

Laphroaig is made by first steeping the barley in soft, peaty Islay water and allowing it to germinate, which involves raking and turning it by hand on the malting floor for six days. The germinated barley is then dried in a swirling peat fire, and it's the smoke from this pungent Islay peat that gives Laphroaig its distinctive "peaty reek" character. After distillation the whisky is matured in Kentucky oak casks, racked in the maturation sheds on the seashore (right of photograph). Here it is washed by the cool, salty wind from the Atlantic, and on a stormy night the sea has been known to enter the sheds, swirling beneath the barrels. It's no surprise,

therefore, that Laphroaig's unique, peaty taste also carries a strong hint of iodine and sharp, salty Atlantic air.

It is styled "the definitive Islay malt whisky" because it epitomises the taste of Islay – rich, smoky, peaty and full of character. It is a whisky that releases the pungent, earthy aroma of blue peat smoke, the sweet nuttiness of the barley and the delicate, heathery perfume of Islay's streams. Laphroaig is definitely an acquired taste, but one shared by the HRH Prince of Wales, who awarded Laphroaig his Royal Warrant in 1994 and commissions his own "Highgrove" edition.

Water is drawn from Kilbride Loch, having run over heather-clad granite hills and through acres of peat bogs. The distillery operates original floor maltings and peat kiln, a stainless steel Lauter mash tun, 6 stainless steel washbacks, 3 wash stills, 3 small spirit stills and one larger one, to maintain the balance of flavour.

Laphroaig Single Islay Malt whisky is bottled at 10 years old (profiled), at 15, 30 and 40 years old and at 10 years old cask-strength, the latter non chill-filtered. Special editions include Laphroaig Quarter Cask, matured in tiny oak butts originally designed for smuggling whisky by packhorse. Being small, the oak contributes more to the flavour, which is smooth and delightfully creamy with less pungent peatyness.

The visitor centre is open all year round and offers tours, tastings and a shop. For those not able to get to Islay, the website *laphroaig.com* offers an excellent virtual distillery tour. Devotees can join the "Friends of Laphroaig", which includes a free lifetime's lease on a plot of Islay with annual rent paid in whisky at the distillery. Laphroaig has over 230,000 friends worldwide.

Feature	Profile
●●●●	Body
●●	Sweetness
●●●●	Smoky
●●●●	Medicinal
●	Tobacco
	Honey
	Spicy
●	Winey
●	Nutty
●	Malty
	Fruity
	Floral

Age 10 years
Strength 40%
Nose Pungent, earthy aroma of blue peat smoke
Taste Very peaty, smoky, salty and medicinal with some malty nuttiness
Cluster J Full-bodied, dry, pungent, peaty and medicinal, with spicy, tobacco notes
Similar to Lagavulin, Ardbeg, Caol Ila

175

LINKWOOD

{LINK-*wood*}

Linkwood distillery was built by Peter Brown in 1821 on the River Lossie, near Elgin. The original stone still house and single pagoda-topped malt house have been preserved and are still in use. When it was rebuilt by his son William Brown in 1873, the *Elgin Courant* of 1874 reported that "the aqua it produces is quite equal to that which attained the celebrity of Linkwood whisky". Great care has always been taken to maintain consistency with the original whisky, to the extent that faithful replicas of the original two stills were commissioned in 1971, complete with bumps and dents, so as to safeguard the character of the spirit.

The emblem on the label is a pair of swans, frequent residents of the Linkwood Burn above the dam that collects the cooling water. Process water is drawn from springs near Milbuies Loch. The distillery operates a cast iron copper-topped mash tun, 11 Oregon pine washbacks and 6 stills – 4 in the new extension and 2 in the original still house.

Linkwood Single Malt whisky is available at 12 years old (profiled) in Diageo's Flora and Fauna range, and as Linkwood 1975 Vintage in the Rare Malts range. It is also used in blends which take the bulk of the production.

Linkwood distillery does not have a visitor centre or offer tours.

Feature	Profile
●●	Body
●●●	Sweetness
●	Smoky
	Medicinal
	Tobacco
●	Honey
●	Spicy
●●	Winey
	Nutty
●	Malty
●●●	Fruity
●●	Floral

Age 12 years
Strength 43%
Nose Fragrant and sweet, with a whiff of smoke
Taste Fruity and floral with honey, malt and spice notes
Cluster C Medium-bodied, medium-sweet, with fruity, floral, honey, malty notes and spicy hints
Similar to Glendullan, Glen Elgin, Royal Brackla

SPEYSIDE
SINGLE MALT
SCOTCH WHISKY

LINKWOOD

distillery stands on the *River Lossie*, close to *ELGIN* in *Speyside*. The *distillery* has retained its *traditional atmosphere* since its *establishment* in 1821. Great care *&* has always been taken to *safeguard* the character of the *whisky* which has remained the same through the years. Linkwood is one of the *FINEST & Single Malt Scotch Whiskies* available – *full bodied* with a hint of *sweetness* and a *slightly smoky aroma.*

YEARS **12** OLD

43% vol   Distilled & Bottled in SCOTLAND.
LINKWOOD DISTILLERY
Elgin, Moray, Scotland.   70cl

LOCH LOMOND

{*loch*-LOW-*mond*}

Nestling beside the river Leven at the southernmost tip of Loch Lomond, the distillery takes its name and water from this most picturesque and celebrated of all Scotland's lochs. It is just above the "Highland Line", so its whiskies can be described as Highland. The distillery's most famous fan is Capitaine Haddock, a friend of Tintin, who has been enjoying a glass of Loch Lomond whisky for over 50 years!

The distillery has expanded rapidly and can now produce 4 million litres of spirit a year. It operates a large Lauter mash tun, 18 stainless steel washbacks, and a unique set of stills that can produce several different single malts. It also has a continuous grain still that enables Loch Lomond uniquely to produce single Highland blended whiskies. It has its own cooperage, where oak casks are

crafted, repaired and re-charred. The whisky is matured at the distillery using a range of casks, including some specially selected French wine barrels. The stills include 4 with unusual rectifying heads (pictured), which can be used to increase reflux so that only the lighter volatiles pass into the condenser. When a short

middle cut is taken, the resulting spirit is lighter, whereas longer runs produce a heavier spirit, and hence the character of the resulting whisky can be varied.

Loch Lomond Single Highland Malt whisky is available with no age statement (profiled)and at 21 years old slightly peated; and as Inchmurrin 10 years old un-peated. Other editions in the Distillery Select range include Inchmurrin, Inchmoan, Craiglodge, Croftengea, Glen Douglas and Organic Grain. These whiskies have been profiled by *Whisky Analyst*.

Loch Lomond distillery does not have a visitor centre or offer tours.

Feature	Profile
●	Body
●	Sweetness
●	Smoky
●	Medicinal
	Tobacco
●	Honey
●	Spicy
●	Winey
●	Nutty
●●	Malty
●	Fruity
●●	Floral

Age No age statement
Strength 40%
Nose Scented, minty, summer flowers and brandy butter
Taste Light and quite swett, limes and raisins, with hints of heather honey, Madeira wine and smoke
Cluster E Light, medium-sweet, low peat, with floral, malty notes and fruity, spicy, honey hints
Similar to Bunnahabhain, Glenallachie, Glenburgie

LONGMORN

*{long-*MORN}

Longmorn, or Lhanmorgund in Gaelic, means the "place of the holy man" because the distillery is on the site of the ancient chapel of St. Marnoch. It was built in 1894 by John Duff, who also built its sister distillery BenRiach, both of which were linked to the railway. Longmorn Station is retained as a feature, as are a Victorian water wheel and a steam engine.

Longmorn is an attractive Victorian sandstone distillery, with a pagoda-topped chimney, that nestles below Blackhills. The emblem on its bottle is an osprey, a bird which has recently returned to the Spey forests after being hunted to the point of extinction.

Its malted barley is supplied lightly peated to order by maltsters, and its water is drawn from the peaty burnside springs that rise in the Blackhills. It operates a stainless steel mash tun, 8 stainless steel washbacks and 8 small pot stills. The whisky is matured in a mixture of ex-bourbon American oak and European sherry casks. Production is quite high at 3.5 million litres a year, most of which goes for blending.

The stills were directly heated by coal fires until 1993, with rummagers to remove burnt solids and burnish the interiors. This increases the exposure of the low wines to copper and thus enhances the richness of the spirit. The present malts were produced before the distillery converted to steam heating, using malted barley produced from the traditional floor maltings at BenRiach next door, with peat cut from Mannoch Hill. This explains why some of the malts are distinctly smoky. It will be interesting to see whether the flavour of the whisky changes significantly in the future.

Longmorn Highland Single Malt whisky is available at 15 years old (profiled), and at 17 years old cask strength, non chill-filtered. Vintage

The Longmorn workforce of 1914 with an original steam engine in the background.

Feature	Profile
●●●	Body
●●	Sweetness
●	Smoky
	Medicinal
	Tobacco
●	Honey
●	Spicy
●	Winey
●●●	Nutty
●●●	Malty
●●	Fruity
●●●	Floral

Age 15 years
Strength 45%
Nose Aromatic, floral and honeyed. Some sherry and spice discernible
Taste Full-bodied, floral and fruity with malty caramel notes, a touch of sherried spice and smoke
Cluster B Medium-bodied, medium-sweet, with nutty, malty, floral, honey and fruity notes
Similar to Edradour, Strathisla, Scapa

editions are available from Gordon & MacPhail, Signatory and others. It is used in Chivas blends, such as Chivas Regal and in Seagram's Heritage Selection. Longmorn is a great malt made in the traditional way.

Longmorn distillery does not have a visitor centre or offer tours.

181

MACALLAN

{*ma*-CALLAN}

Macallan distillery was one of the first to be founded in Speyside. It was licensed in 1824 to Alexander Reid but, as was often the case at that period, whisky had already been produced on the farm for years. Its water originally came from Ringorm Burn, but today it is drawn from four boreholes by the River Spey, and the company owns a mile-long stretch of the River Spey to protect the supply. It also owns Easter Elchies House, pictured, built in 1700 by a Captain Grant and sensitively restored in 1986.

The distillery uses unpeated malted barley including a proportion of low yield *Golden Promise*, a traditional variety which they claim maintains the high quality, flavour and consistency of their whiskies. It operates a stainless steel mash tun, 16 stainless steel wash-backs, 5 wash stills and 10 spirit stills. The wash stills are directly heated by gas fires, with rummagers to remove burnt solids and burnish the interiors. This increases the exposure of the low wines to copper, thus enhancing the flavour of the whisky. At 1,500 litres capacity they are the smallest to be directly heated by fires beneath. Macallan whiskies have been matured extensively in Spanish oak sherry casks. These are specially selected in Jerez, having been prepared with dry

oloroso sherry for up to two years. However, in a bid to extend their market, a Macallan Fine Oak range was introduced in 2004 with whisky matured in American ex-bourbon barrels.

Prior to the 1970s, Macallan's production went mainly for blending, whereas today it is sold mostly as single malt whiskies. The company wisely decided to set aside stock for marketing as a single malt, starting in 1974 with a budget of £25 for an advert in a local paper. Today "The Macallan" ranks amongst the five best-selling malt whiskies in the world. Indeed it is a tribute to their success that many other distillers have tried to enter Macallan's sherried-malt market, with a myriad of special wine finishes.

Our featured malt is Macallan 10 years old in the Sherry Oak range, which was chosen in 2001 by Michael Martin MP as the House of Commons Speaker's Malt. Other bottlings are at 12, 18, 25 and 30 years old, and Macallan Elegancia 12 years old, which was the first to be modified with whisky from bourbon casks. Macallan Fine Oak is bottled at 8, 10, 12, 15, 18, 21, 25 and 30 years old. These are markedly different to the Sherry Oak editions, which just goes to prove that the cask has the most important influence on the flavour of the whisky. A set of Macallan Travel malts, supposedly reflecting the style of the Twenties, Thirties, Forties and Fifties are both intriguing and affordable. Somewhat less affordable are the Macallan Fine and Rare vintages, ranging from 1937 to 1975, and a replica of an 1876 vintage – *themacallan.com* has all the latest information.

The Gardener's Cottage Visitor Centre is open all year, offering tours, tastings and a shop. Special tutored tastings are also available, by appointment.

Feature	Profile
●●●●	Body
●●●	Sweetness
●	Smoky
	Medicinal
	Tobacco
●●	Honey
●	Spicy
●●●●	Winey
●●	Nutty
●●	Malty
●●●	Fruity
●	Floral

Age 10 years
Strength 40%
Nose Toffee sweet with dried fruits, cloves and sherry
Taste Smooth and well-rounded fruity flavour with honeyed sherry and oak evident, and a whiff of smoke
Cluster A Full-bodied, medium-sweet, pronounced sherry with fruity, spicy, malty notes and nutty, smoky hints
Similar to Glendronach, Royal Lochnagar, Dailuaine

MANNOCHMORE

{*man-och*-MORE}

Mannochmore distillery was built in 1971 on the same site as Glenlossie distillery, and was originally intended to produce Haig blends. It is a large, modern complex that lacks character, but has a high production capacity. The emblem on the bottle is a greater spotted woodpecker, and these can sometimes be heard drilling in the Millbusies Woods nearby.

The distillery draws its process water from the Bardon Burn, and cooling water from the Gedloch Burn. It operates a cast iron mash tun, 8 larch washbacks and 6 steam-heated stills. At one time the distillery also produced an undistinguished Loch Dhu black whisky, using a special double-charred cask preparation process, but this has since ceased being issued.

Mannochmore Single Malt whisky is available at 12 years old (profiled) in Diageo's Flora and Fauna range, and as Mannochmore 1974 Vintage in the "Rare Malts" range. It is used in Haig and Dimple blends, which account for the bulk of its production.

Mannochmore distillery does not have a visitor centre or offer tours.

Feature	Profile
●●	Body
●	Sweetness
●	Smoky
	Medicinal
	Tobacco
●	Honey
●	Spicy
●	Winey
●●	Nutty
●	Malty
●●	Fruity
●●	Floral

Age 12 years
Strength 43%
Nose Light, aromatic and floral
with a hint of smoke
Taste Fruity and creamy, with
hints of honey, oak and spice
Cluster D Light, medium-
sweet, low or no peat, with
fruity, floral, malty notes and
nutty hints
Similar to Speyside, Aultmore,
Glen Grant

SPEYSIDE
SINGLE MALT *SCOTCH WHISKY*

MANNOCHMORE

distillery stands a few miles *south* of Elgin in *Morayshire*. The nearby
Millbuie Woods are rich in birdlife, including the Great *Spotted Woodpecker*.
The *distillery* draws process *water* from the Bardon Burn,
which has its *source* in the MANNOCH HILLS, and *cooling water* from
the *Gedloch* Burn and the *Burn of Foths*. Mannochmore *single*
MALT WHISKY has a *light, fruity* aroma and a *smooth, mellow* taste

AGED **12** YEARS

MILTONDUFF

{*mill-ton*-DUFF}

Miltonduff distillery was established in 1824 by Andrew Pearey and Donald Bain, near the Benedictine Priory of Pluscarden, beside the Black Burn. Alfred Barnard recorded that in the fifteenth century the Black Burn was blessed by the Abbot of Pluscarden, and the life-giving beverage distilled therefrom was thus christened "*aqua vitae*". This was an area rich in illicit distillation. At the beginning of the eighteenth century there were more than 50 unlicensed stills here, because the hills form a triangle that allowed a mutual signalling system to warn of any approaching Excise officers.

The distillery draws its water from the Black Burn which flows through the peat of Black Hill. It operates a stainless steel mash tun, 16 stainless steel washbacks and 6 stills. Hiram Walker rebuilt it in 1975, installing 2 Lomond stills that have since been removed. The whisky is matured in American bourbon oak casks and refills, stored in warehouses at the distillery.

Miltonduff Single Highland Malt whisky is available at 15 years old (profiled), and from Gordon & MacPhail. The whisky is used in various blends, notably Ballantine's.

The distillery does not have a visitor centre or offer tours.

Feature	Profile
●●	Body
●●●●	Sweetness
●	Smoky
	Medicinal
	Tobacco
●	Honey
	Spicy
	Winey
●●	Nutty
●	Malty
●	Fruity
●●	Floral

Age 15 years
Strength 46%
Nose Sweet, with a hint of honey and a whiff of smoke
Taste Very sweet with nutty, floral notes, and some fruit and honey
Cluster G Medium-bodied, sweet, low peat and floral notes
Similar to Dufftown, Speyburn, Glen Spey

MORTLACH

{MORT-*lack*}

Mortlach distillery was built on the site of an illicit still in the early nineteenth century and, in 1823, was licensed to James Findlater, the first legal distiller in Dufftown. Its water was originally drawn from Highland John's Well, a source disputed with Dufftown distillery, but today it is supplied by springs in the Conval Hills. William Grant worked here for twenty years as a clerk, before leaving to build Glenfiddich distillery nearby in 1886. The emblem on the Mortlach bottle is the shy goosander, a crested duck that nests and fishes on the River Dullan.

The distillery was expanded in 1897 when a private railway line, shared with Glendullan distillery, was installed linking it to Dufftown Station. It was fully modernised in the 1990s, and now operates a stainless steel Lauter mash tun, 6 Oregon pine washbacks and 6 steam-heated copper stills of unusual differing shapes. Cooling is by 6 exterior copper worm tubs, the lyne pipes feeding into a large serpentine coil that becomes progressively narrower as it progresses down the tub. The cooling water rising up the tub ensures that it is coldest at the end of the process. This slow, gentle way of condensing the spirit, extending its reflux with the copper, combined with slow fermentation of up to four days, contributes to the fine flavour and character of the resulting spirit. The whisky is matured in sherry casks for 16 years, which accounts for its pronounced sherry flavour and its classification alongside Macallan.

Mortlach malt whisky, or "Mortie" as it is known locally, is one of Diageo's best kept secrets. It was denied its rightful place in their "Classic Malts of Scotland" range, and virtually all the production is used for blending, notably in Johnnie Walker. However, the malt can be obtained in Diageo's Flora and Fauna range at 16 years old (profiled), and in the Rare Malts range 1971 vintage. Other versions are available from Gordon & MacPhail, Signatory and other independents.

Mortlach distillery does not have a visitor centre or offer tours.

Feature	Profile
●●●	Body
●●	Sweetness
●●	Smoky
	Medicinal
	Tobacco
●●	Honey
●●●	Spicy
●●●	Winey
●●	Nutty
●	Malty
●●	Fruity
●●	Floral

Age 16 years
Strength 43%
Nose Fruity, smoky and aromatic
Taste Full-bodied with pronounced sherry, honey and spice notes. Well-balanced fruity flavour and finish
Cluster A Full-bodied, medium-sweet, pronounced sherry with fruity, spicy, malty notes and nutty, smoky hints
Similar to Royal Lochnagar, Dailuaine, Glendronach

SPEYSIDE
SINGLE MALT
SCOTCH WHISKY

MORTLACH

was the first of seven
distilleries in Dufftown. In the
C19th farm animals kept in
adjoining byres were fed on
barley left over from processing
Today water from springs in
the CONVAL HILLS is used to
produce this delightful
smooth, fruity single
MALT SCOTCH WHISKY.

AGED 16 YEARS

Distilled & Bottled in SCOTLAND.
MORTLACH DISTILLERY
Dufftown, Keith, Banffshire, Scotland.

43% vol   70 cl

189

OBAN

{OH-*bun*}

ban, Gaelic for the "little bay of caves", is a sheltered harbour town in the West Highlands. It is the gateway to the Isles and is steeped in Viking and Gaelic history. The distillery was founded in 1794 by Hugh Stevenson, a local merchant and entrepreneur, and is situated in the heart of the old town. It is the oldest and smallest of the Classic Malts distilleries, nestling in the heart of the town below McCaig's Tower (pictured). It was rebuilt in 1890–94 by J. Walter Higgin and, during excavation, a cave containing human bones and artefacts dating from the Mesolithic era (4,500–3,000 BC) was discovered in the Creag a'Bharrain cliffs behind the distillery. The distillery draws its water from Loch Gleann a'Bhearraidh and operates a small stainless steel mash tun, 4 European larch washbacks and 2 lampglass-shaped stills. The stills, which are amongst the smallest in Scotland, have unusually short lyne arms due to the cramped space of the still house. The relatively high contact with copper, due to the size of the stills and the use of traditional copper worm condensers, creates a rich spirit that has lots of character. Oban Single West Highland Malt is matured in American oak bourbon casks, resulting in a whisky that displays the subtle character of the spirit unmasked by excessive cask or peat flavours. The featured malt is Oban 14 years old in Diageo's Classic Malts range. Oban Single Malts are also available at 20 years old, 32 years old, and in

Oban Distillers Editions finished in Montilla Fino Sherry casks, which impart flavours of 'sweet tobacco' and 'peach'.

The visitor centre in the former maltings has been completely redesigned, winning a five-star tourism rating. It is open all year and has an exhibition and audio-visual presentation about the history and growth of the town and its distillery. Tours of the distillery and tastings are available.

Feature	Profile
●●	Body
●●	Sweetness
●●	Smoky
●●	Medicinal
	Tobacco
	Honey
●●	Spicy
	Winey
●●	Nutty
●●	Malty
●●	Fruity
	Floral

Age 14 years
Strength 43%
Nose Salty, malty and sweet, with a discernible smokiness
Taste Rich, medium-bodied, quite sweet and peaty with citric fruits, dried figs, honey and spices evident
Cluster H Medium-bodied, medium-sweet, with smoky, fruity, spicy notes and floral, nutty hints
Similar to Balblair, Craigellachie, Old Pulteney

OLD PULTENEY

{*old*-PULT-*nay*}

Pulteney distillery is in Wick, on a rugged, windswept, sea-pounded bay surrounded by ancient ruined castles. Wick is the Viking name for an opening or bay.

Founded in 1826, it is named after Sir William Johnson Pulteney who commissioned Thomas Telford to build a major new herring fishing town, harbour and distillery at the estuary of Wick River during the 19th century herring boom. The distillery is the most northerly on the Scottish mainland and was quite inaccessible when established, except by sea. Wick became one of the world's busiest herring fishing ports and many of the distillery workers were also fishermen. Over 10,000 people were employed in the herring industry and a thousand boats could be harboured at Wick (page 14). Many a dram of Old Pulteney was savoured when the fleet was in and the kippers were smoking. The distillery has played a prominent role in the community and the sea breeze and salty air are evident in the taste of Old Pulteney. This association is also celebrated by the emblem on the bottle – a nineteenth-century herring fishing boat.

The distillery draws its process water from Hempriggs Loch and uses un-peated malted barley. It operates a cast iron mash tun, 6 stainless steel washbacks and 2 stills. The wash still is called "Smuggler's Kettle" because of its unique shape. The distinctively concentrated flavour of Old Pulteney whisky may be partly attributed to the use of a purifier above the spirit still. Pulteney distillery is one of the few remaining distilleries to use traditional copper worm tubs for condensing. The whisky is matured in a selection of ex-bourbon American oak casks and ex-sherry butts at the distillery.

It has been dubbed the "Manzanilla of the North" for its uniquely salty and beguilingly complex aroma. Old Pulteney Single Malt whisky is available at 12 years old (profiled), at 17 and 21 years old non chill-filtered, and it is

used in Old Pulteney Liqueur. Visitors to the distillery can fill, seal and date their own bottle of Old Pulteney malt whisky, drawn directly from a single cask.

The visitor centre and shop are open all year. The tour includes a presentation of the seafaring history of Wick and its distillery, and is finished off with a whisky tasting. For further information visit *oldpulteney.com*.

Feature	Profile
●●	Body
●	Sweetness
●●	Smoky
●●	Medicinal
●	Tobacco
	Honey
●	Spicy
●	Winey
●●	Nutty
●●	Malty
●●	Fruity
●●	Floral

Age 12 years
Strength 40%
Nose Delicate light aroma, grassy with a whiff of the North Sea
Taste Medium-dry, with great complexity, apples, vanilla, chocolate and cake, and a whiff of smoke
Cluster H Medium-bodied, medium-sweet, with smoky, fruity, spicy notes and floral, nutty hints
Similar to Craigellachie, Oban, Glenmorangie

ROYAL BRACKLA

{*royal*-BRACK-*la*}

oyal Brackla distillery was built in 1812 by Captain William Fraser on the Cawdor estate, which is the setting for Shakespeare's *Macbeth, Thane of Cawdor*. At the time the district was notorious for illicit whisky production, so much so that Captain Fraser complained that he was surrounded by people who drank nothing but whisky, yet he could not sell 100 gallons in a year. In 1835 William IV granted Brackla a Royal warrant – the first distillery to enjoy this distinction – proclaiming it to be his favourite whisky. At that time it became known as "Royal Brackla" or "The King's Own Whisky". The warrant was renewed by Queen Victoria in 1838, for it is indeed a whisky fit for Sovereign and Thane.

The distillery was modernised in 1965, extended in 1970 and further improved in 1997. It draws its process water from the Cursack Springs above Cawdor Castle, and its cooling water from Cawdor Burn and uses lightly peated malted barley supplied to order. It operates a large stainless steel mash tun, 2 stainless steel washbacks, and 4 large stills. The whisky is largely matured in ex-bourbon American oak casks with some sherry casks being used for the malts.

Royal Brackla was sold with the Dewar's portfolio to Bacardi in 1998, hence its malt whisky was distilled by the previous owners, who used lightly peated barley to give the whisky a slightly smoky note. In future the whiskies are likely to be less peaty than the present version.

Royal Brackla Highland Single Malt is available at 10 years old (profiled) and at vintage bottlings in Gordon & MacPhail's Connoiseurs Choice

Feature	Profile
●●	Body
●●●	Sweetness
●●	Smoky
●	Medicinal
●	Tobacco
●	Honey
●●	Spicy
●	Winey
	Nutty
●●	Malty
●●●	Fruity
●●	Floral

Age 10 years
Strength 40%
Nose Fresh, floral and grassy, with a whiff of smoke
Taste Sweet and creamy, with lots of fruit, malt and oaky vanilla, and aniseed in the finish
Cluster C Medium-bodied, medium-sweet, with fruity, floral, honey, malty notes and spicy hints
Similar to Benriach, Linkwood, Glen Ord

Range, Signatory and other independents. It is used in Dewar's White Label blend, which accounts for the bulk of its production.

The distillery does not have a visitor centre or offer tours.

ROYAL
BRACKLA

Highland Single Malt

SCOTCH WHISKY

The ROYAL BRACKLA DISTILLERY lies between the River Findhorn and the Moray Firth at Cawdor, not far from Nairn. FOUNDED IN 1812 by Captain William Fraser of Brackla House, Brackla was the first distillery to be granted a ROYAL WARRANT in 1835 by King William IV. At that time it became known as 'Royal Brackla' or "THE KING'S OWN WHISKY".

AGED **10** YEARS

70cl 40% vol

DISTILLED AND BOTTLED IN SCOTLAND
ROYAL BRACKLA DISTILLERY,
CAWDOR, NAIRN.
FROM THE HOUSE OF DEWAR.

ROYAL LOCHNAGAR

{*royal*-LOCH-*na*-GAR}

Situated in a spectacular setting beside the River Dee, close to the Royal Palace of Balmoral, Royal Lochnagar distillery is a Highland gem. It was built in 1845 on a farm and it retains a farmyard atmosphere to this day. In 1848, the manager John Begg wrote to Prince Albert, inviting him to sample his new whisky, and was surprised when the Prince arrived without warning together with Queen Victoria and the royal children. The Queen and Prince Albert toured the distillery and sampled their first dram and the royal warrant was quickly granted, one of the fastest on record. The whisky has been enjoyed by generations of the Royal Family and their Balmoral staff for over 150 years. Indeed, it was Queen Victoria's enthusiasm for whisky, following her visit to the distillery, that helped create the international demand for "Scotch".

Royal Lochnagar's open-topped mash tun and 2 elegant onion-shaped stills, like upturned wine glasses, are much the same as in Victorian times, though the distillery and visitor centre have been modernised. Process water is drawn from springs on the lower slopes of Lochnagar Mountain. The distillery uses lightly peated barley and operates 3 Oregon pine washbacks with unusually long 80–100 hours fermentation times. The output from both stills is condensed using traditional worm condensers in cast-iron tanks outside the stillhouse. These are run hot, to extend the time that the vapour is in contact with the copper and thus lighten the spirit. The whisky is matured in American bourbon casks and European oak sherry butts, stored in warehouses at the site. The use of refill casks helps to balance the character of the spirit, which is carefully maintained, against minimal wood

Feature	Profile
●●●	Body
●●	Sweetness
●●	Smoky
	Medicinal
	Tobacco
●●	Honey
●●	Spicy
●●	Winey
●●	Nutty
●●	Malty
●●●	Fruity
●	Floral

Age 12 years
Strength 40%
Nose Aromatic, grassy, with rich spicy fruit
Taste Complex, layered flavours of butterscotch and rich fruit cake, with honey, sherry and spice also discernable
Cluster A Full-bodied, medium-sweet, pronounced sherry with fruity, spicy, malty notes and nutty, smoky hints
Similar to Glendronach, Dailuaine, Dalmore

influences. Royal Lochnagar Single Highland Malt whisky is available at 12 years old (profiled), in a limited edition "Special Selected Reserve" and in Diageo's Rare Malts range at 30 years old. It is also used in blends such as Johnnie Walker (Black and Blue Labels) and Vat 69.

The distillery runs trade courses and is the seat of learning for Diageo. Its visitor centre is open all year. Visitors can enjoy a guided tour, sample the Royal dram and purchase the full range of Diageo malts in the shop.

SCAPA

{SCAPP-*ah*}

Scapa distillery was built in 1885 by John Townsend beside the Lingro Burn on the shore of Scapa Flow. It is a natural harbour that links the North Sea to the Atlantic Ocean and was used as a naval base in both World Wars. Orkney is an island steeped in history with almost 3,000 relics, such as Neolithic standing stones, chambered tombs, Iron Age earth houses, a Viking palace and early Celtic monasteries. A fortified Broch tower dating from 3000 BC stands close to the distillery, and the graves of Norse warriors, buried with their swords and horses, have been found nearby. When he visited the distillery in 1886, Alfred Barnard noted the Broch as "undoubtedly the most interesting class of Scottish antiquities" and he was moved by the beautiful sea-scape below, sparkling in the bright sunshine. The German fleet was scuttled in Scapa Flow in 1918 at the end of World War I,

and in World War II the distillery was saved from fire by the Royal Navy.

Two of the original Victorian warehouses survive, but most of the present buildings date from 1959, when it was substantially rebuilt, and a new stillhouse was added in 2004. In the midst of its ancient history, the modern Scapa distillery looms incongruously above the shore in an area of great natural beauty. It was once powered by a water wheel and this has been retained as a feature.

The distillery draws its hard, peaty water from the Lingro Burn and, to compensate, it uses totally unpeated malted barley. It operates a squat Lomond wash still with a short cylindrical neck and a more conventional spirit still. The whisky is matured in ex-bourbon American oak casks in warehouses beside the sea.

Scapa Single Orkney Malt whisky is available at 14 years old (profiled) and

Feature	Profile
●●	Body
●●	Sweetness
●	Smoky
●	Medicinal
	Tobacco
●●	Honey
●	Spicy
●	Winey
●●	Nutty
●●	Malty
●●	Fruity
●●	Floral

Age 14 years
Strength 40%
Nose Floral and delicate, grassy, burnt toast and cedar wood notes and a whiff of sea air
Taste Medium-dry and peppery, heather honey, vanilla, pistachios and toffee
Cluster B Medium-bodied, medium-sweet, with nutty, malty, floral, honey and fruity notes
Similar to Aberfeldy Benromach, Knockando

at 25 years old. Other versions are available in Gordon & MacPhail's Island Malt Range.

The distillery does not have a visitor centre, but visitors are welcome by appointment.

SPEYBURN

{*spey*-BURN}

There are many beautifully situated distilleries in Scotland, but few can surpass Speyburn, sitting majestically in a corner of the Spey Valley at the foot of the densely wooded hills, on the outskirts of the quiet Highland town of Rothes. Designed by the famous architect, Charles Doig of Elgin, it is reputed to be the most photographed distillery in Scotland. The site was chosen for its proximity to the Great North of Scotland railway and the plentiful supply of clear spring water. It sits below Cnock na Croiche, the "hillock of the gibbet", where Rothes criminals were hanged.

The most distinctive features are its 2- and 3-storey buildings, which use the sloping site to best effect. With its impressive elevations and traditional pagoda chimney, Speyburn still commands an imposing aspect in the Glen of Rothes. The distillery draws its soft peaty water from the Granty Burn, a tributary of the river Spey, and uses unpeated malted barley. It operates a stainless steel copper-domed mash tun, 6 Oregon pine washbacks, and 2 stills. The stone-built wash room is exceptionally cold, which allows for a slower and better fermentation. It still uses worm tub condensers, which allow longer contact with copper and hence extended catalysis, resulting in a sweeter, more floral spirit. The whisky is matured in ex-bourbon American oak casks at the distillery and it was the first to install steam-powered drum maltings. The emblem on the label is a leaping salmon, a native of the Spey, which is famous for its salmon fishing.

Speyburn Single Highland Malt whisky is available at 10 years old (profiled), at 21 years old as a single-cask limited edition and at 27 years old in the Highland selection series. It does not have a visitor centre, but visitors are welcome by appointment.

Feature	Profile
●●	Body
●●●●	Sweetness
●	Smoky
	Medicinal
	Tobacco
●●	Honey
●	Spicy
	Winey
	Nutty
●●	Malty
●	Fruity
●●	Floral

Age 10 years
Strength 40%
Nose Fresh, aromatic and malty, with a touch of smoke
Taste Medium-bodied and sweet, with a toffee, oaky note and a fruity finish
Cluster G Medium-bodied, sweet, low peat and floral notes
Similar to Miltonduff, Glenfiddich, Dufftown

SPEYSIDE

{*spey*-SIDE}

Speyside distillery is located near picturesque Kingussie, on the banks of the River Tromie, which feeds into the River Spey. It is one of Scotland's newest distilleries, the dream of its founder, George Christie, and it was hand-built by Alex Fairlie, a dry stane dyker on the site of one of the oldest barley mills in Scotland.

Construction started in 1962 and finished in 1989, but it was not until 1991 that the first spirit began to flow. The distillery draws its water from the River Tromie and only uses *Chariot* barley, lightly peated and malted to order. It operates a stainless steel mash tun, 4 stainless steel washbacks and 2 small pot stills. The smallness of the stills maximises contact with the copper and hence catalysis, resulting in a rich, fruity spirit. The whisky is matured in ex-bourbon American oak hogsheads, with a few European oak sherry butts to

provide a sherried edge for the malts.

A tautology arising from naming a distillery "Speyside", even one that lies directly beside the river Spey, is that "Speyside Single Speyside Malt" does not trip neatly off the tongue. Therefore, it is called Speyside Single Highland Malt whisky, which really goes to prove the point that classifying whiskies by region is somewhat nonsensical.

Speyside Single Highland Malt whisky is available at 12 years old (profiled), and in Glentromie 12 years old and 17 years old vatted malts, and Drumguish and Great Glen, which bear no age statement. The company also produces five blended whiskies under their Speyside label, ranging from 15 to 30 years old, a Speyside Millennium 2000 edition, and two Glentromie blends. The whisky also appeared in the BBC's "Monarch of the Glen" series as the Laird of Glenbogle's favourite malt.

Feature	Profile
●●	Body
●●	Sweetness
●	Smoky
	Medicinal
	Tobacco
●	Honey
	Spicy
●	Winey
●●	Nutty
●●	Malty
●●	Fruity
●●	Floral

Age 12 years
Strength 40%
Nose Fragrant, sweet and malty with a whiff of smoke
Taste Medium-bodied, creamy with fruity and floral notes, some nuts and vanilla
Cluster D Light, medium-sweet, low or no peat, with fruity, floral, malty notes and nutty hints
Similar to Aultmore, Arran, Tamdhu

Speyside distillery does not have a visitor centre or offer tours. Kingussie is well worth visiting, however, as is the nearby ruin of Ruthven Barracks, built by the English army to control the Highlanders after the 1715 rebellion. You can take a virtual tour at *speysidedistillery.co.uk*.

SPRINGBANK

*{spring-*BANK}

Springbank distillery was first licensed in 1828, but is said to have been previously operated as an illicit still by Archibald Mitchell. It is still owned by the same family and is, therefore, the oldest independent distillery in Scotland. Springbank uniquely carries out all of the production process, from traditional floor maltings to bottling, at the one site. It is the only remaining distillery to malt all its barley on a traditional malting floor.

Water is drawn from Crosshill Loch, fed by springs on Beinn Ghuilean. The distillery operates a century-old cast iron mash tun, 6 boatskin larch washbacks, and 3 medium-sized pot stills. The wash still is directly heated with rummagers to remove burnt solids and burnish the interiors. This increases the charring effect of direct flame heating and the exposure of the low wines to copper, thereby enhancing the flavour. Another unusual feature is that some spirit is partly triple-distilled, the low wines, foreshots and feints being re-distilled with the next batch of low wines in an intermediate still before final distillation occurs in the spirit still. This produces a light spirit, but this is not as evident in the Springbank malts as it is in other triple-distilled whiskies. The whiskies are bottled at 46% or cask strength without being chill-filtered to retain the full character of the spirit. They are mainly matured in bourbon casks, with some sherry, rum and port casks used for added complexity or special wood expressions.

Springbank distillery produces three very different malt whiskies. Springbank Campbeltown Single Malt whisky is available at 10 years old (profiled), at 10 years old 100° proof, and at 15, 21, 25 and 32 years old. Longrow single malt 10 years old is double-distilled and heavily peated, and is also available at 10 years old 100° proof, at 14 years old and as Longrow 1995 Tokaji finish. Hazelburn single malt 8 years old, triple-

distilled unpeated sold out in days, but will be repeated. There are also two Springbank blends, Mitchell's 12 years old and Campbeltown Loch.

It does not have a visitor centre, but tours can be arranged in the summer by appointment. There is a shop, Eaglesome, in Campbeltown and you can join the Springbank Society for news and special offers at *springbankdistillers.com*.

STRATHISLA

{strath-EYE-la}

S et in the medieval market town of Keith, on the banks of the River Isla, Strathisla distillery claims to be the oldest in the Highlands. It was founded in 1786 by George Taylor and Alexander Milne as Milton distillery, named after nearby Milton Castle. With its distinctive twin pagodas, cobbled courtyard, water wheel and classic, gabled granite buildings, Strathisla is one of the prettiest of the traditional distilleries and well worth visiting.

Much of its production goes for blending, and Strathisla has been dubbed the "home and heart of Chivas Regal". Its water is drawn from Broomhill Spring, a source recorded by Dominican monks in the twelfth century. It operates a stainless steel mash tun, 10 Oregon pine washbacks and 4 compact, copper pot stills, crammed into an atmospheric oak-beamed still house, and 2 delightfully original spirit safes. The stills have lyne arms that incline at different angles which, together with their squat size, means that heavier alchols reach the condensers, resulting in a richer, more complex spirit. The whisky is matured in a mixture of American oak ex-bourbon and European sherry casks in dunnage warehouses at the distillery.

Strathisla single malt whisky is available at 12 years old (profiled) and at 15, 25 and 35 years old cask strength, non chill-filtered. Several other editions are available from Gordon & MacPhail and Signatory. It is used in several blends such as Chivas Regal 12, 18, 21 and 30 years old, Royal Salute "100 cask" selection, 100 Pipers, Chivas Revolve 1801 and Passport.

The visitor centre and shop are open all year. Visitors are welcomed in the Isla room with a video presentation and a glass of Chivas Regal 12 years old, followed by a tour of the distillery and a taste of Chivas Regal 18 years old or Strathisla 12 years old.

Feature	Profile
●●	Body
●●	Sweetness
●	Smoky
	Medicinal
	Tobacco
●●	Honey
●●	Spicy
●●	Winey
●●●	Nutty
●●●	Malty
●●●	Fruity
●●	Floral

Age 12 years
Strength 43%
Nose Meadows, citrus fruit and spice, and a hint of peat
Taste Medium-bodied, medium sweet with apricots, almonds honey notes and a spicy finish
Cluster B Medium-bodied, medium-sweet, with nutty, malty, floral, honey and fruity notes
Similar to Benromach, Aberfeldy, Blair Athol

STRATHMILL

{*strath*-MILL}

Strathmill distillery was converted from a former flour mill in 1891, at a time of great optimism in the industry, when foreign markets were opening to whisky. It was initially named Glenisla-Glenlivet, and was renamed Strathmill in 1895. The flour mill is believed to have existed since 1823, and there are conflicting reports that it might have been used for distilling at some period, probably illicit. Although modernised and extended in the 1960s, it retains some of the original Victorian buildings in a delightful setting beside the River Isla, on the edge of Keith.

It draws its water from a spring above the distillery that flows into the Isla, and its malted barley is supplied lightly peated, to order. The distillery operates a stainless steel mash tun, 6 stainless steel washbacks and 4 squat stills. The spirit stills are fitted with "purifiers" that return the heavier fusel oils to the distillation, allowing only the lighter vapours to continue to reach the condenser. This results in a lighter and cleaner spirit.

The whisky is matured in American oak bourbon and refill casks stored in traditional dunnage warehouses at the distillery. The emblem on the bottle

Feature	Profile
●●	Body
●●●	Sweetness
●	Smoky
	Medicinal
	Tobacco
	Honey
●●	Spicy
	Winey
●●	Nutty
●	Malty
●●●	Fruity
●●	Floral

Age 12 years
Strength 43%
Nose Sweet and fragrant, with a malty note
Taste Medium bodied, sweet with apples and citrus fruits, quite nutty and spicy
Cluster H Medium-bodied, medium-sweet, with smoky, fruity, spicy notes and floral, nutty hints
Similar to Balblair, Glenmorangie, Tamnavulin

is a pied wagtail, which can be seen hunting on the banks of the Isla and occasionally in the distillery yard.

Strathmill Single Highland Malt whisky is available at 12 years old in Diageo's Flora and Fauna series, and occasionally from independents. Most of the production goes for blending, principally in Diageo's J&B blend and formerly in Alfred Dunhill's Old Master and Gentleman's Speyside blends.

Strathmill distillery does not have a visitor centre or offer tours.

SPEYSIDE
SINGLE MALT *SCOTCH WHISKY*

STRATHMILL

distillery was established in 1891 in *a converted grain mill.*
The *PIED WAGTAIL is a* familiar sight in the *distillery yard on*
the banks *of the nearby RIVER ISLA, which provides water*
for cooling. A spring on the site provides *processing water.*
This *deep amber, single MALT* has a light, *rounded body, a* crisp
sweet flavour, with a *dry finish* and *chocolaty aftertaste.*

45%vol   A G E D **12** Y E A R S

TALISKER

{TAL-*is-ker*}

Talisker is the only distillery on the island of Skye – the Misty Isle. It was built in 1830 by Hugh and Kenneth MacAskill, in the Gaelic heartland of Carbost, against the fierce protestations of the kirk Minister, the Rev. Roderick Macleod. He declared this to be "one of the greatest curses that… could befall [this] or any other place".

The distillery stands on the rocky, storm-lashed shore of Loch Harport, in the shadow of the rugged Cuillin Mountains. It was destroyed by fire in 1960, when a valve on the spirit still was accidentally left open and burning spirit ran down the Carbost Burn into Loch Harport, setting the loch itself on fire. It was rebuilt in 1962 and further renovated in 1998. It now boasts a large stainless steel mash tun with a sparkling copper top, 6 Oregon pine washbacks, 3 low wines stills, 2 wash stills with unique U-shaped lyne arms, a fine spirit

safe, and 5 copper worm tubs condensers.

Prior to 1998 the water supply from the Carbost Burn was frequently insufficient in periods of drought. The dam was, therefore, extended and, with the help of a water diviner, some new springs were connected. The mineral-rich water, from these springs on Cnoc nan Speireag (the "Hawk Hill"), that supplies the distillery, runs through heather and peat, which no doubt contribute to the whisky's robust character. The whisky is matured in American bourbon oak casks, plus a few European oloroso sherry butts used for double maturation.

Talisker has been available as a single malt whisky since the late nineteenth century – it was praised by Robert Louis Stevenson in 1880 as "the King o' Drinks", and was bought regularly by the Indian Army. Our featured malt, Talisker 10 years old in Diageo's Classic Malts range, has won several awards in the International Wine and Spirits Competition and International Spirits Challenge. Talisker single malts are also available at 18 years old, at 20 years old and in Talisker Distillers' Edition 1991 finished in Amoroso sherry casks. The distillery celebrated its 175th anniversary in 2005 with the launch of Talisker 175, a vatted malt covering the products of 20 years' production.

The visitor centre has an excellent exhibition on the history of the distillery and its location, and is open all year. Unusually, visitors are given a dram to taste before embarking on the distillery tour. From a pagoda-capped gazebo in the gardens the indigenous peregrine falcons and sparrow hawks can be seen. The very lucky may even catch a glimpse of a white-tailed sea eagle soaring over Hawk Hill, and seals basking on the rocks. Visitors can round off their visit with a dram of Talisker and a plate of Loch Harport oysters, said to be the island's harvest and the island's spirit together, in divine harmony.

Feature	Profile
●●●●	Body
●●	Sweetness
●●●	Smoky
●●●	Medicinal
	Tobacco
●	Honey
●●●	Spicy
	Winey
●	Nutty
●●	Malty
●●	Fruity
	Floral

Age 10 years
Strength 45.8%
Nose Slightly sweet, peaty and salty – powerful island aroma
Taste Rich, full-bodied, pungent with sea-shore, barley-malt flavours, peppered spice and dried-fruit notes
Cluster J Full-bodied, dry, pungent, peaty and medicinal, with spicy, tobacco notes
Similar to Ardbeg, Caol Ila, Lagavulin

TAMDHU

{TAM-*doo*}

Tamdhu distillery was built at Knockando village in the boom of 1897 by William Grant, a director of Highland Distillers. The site was chosen for its plentiful supply of clear spring water and proximity to the Great North of Scotland railway line. After the railway closed in the 1960s, Knockando station was converted into a visitor centre for Alfred Dunhill, who used it to promote their blends. The distillery was extended in the 1970s to 6 stills, but it is the Tamdhu maltings that are of most interest. This is the only Speyside distillery that malts its own barley, producing enough to meet its own needs and those of its parent group and several other Speyside distilleries.

The maltings use long concrete trenches, called Saladin boxes, in which the germinating barley is turned mechanically every nine to twelve hours for five days. The floor of the box is perforated and humid air is circulated through the barley to maintain its temperature at 66°C. The whole process is computer controlled, requiring only one operator to supervise several batches simultaneously. Once the barley has germinated, it is dried in hot air

with any specified amount of peat smoke introduced to order, according to the distiller's peating requirements.

The distillery draws its water from a well below the building and the Tamdhu Burn is used for cooling water. It operates a stainless steel mash tun, 9 Oregon pine washbacks and 6 conventional pot stills. The whisky is matured in a

mixture of American bourbon, European sherry and refill casks.

Tamdhu Single Malt whisky is available with no age statement (profiled), and as vintage editions from Gordon & MacPhail, Cadenhead and Signatory. The whisky is used in the Famous Grouse blend, in Famous Grouse Vintage Malt, and in the Alfred Dunhill blends currently popular in America.

Tamdhu visitor centre is not open for tours.

Feature	Profile
●	Body
●●	Sweetness
●	Smoky
	Medicinal
	Tobacco
●●	Honey
	Spicy
●	Winey
●	Nutty
●●	Malty
●●	Fruity
●●	Floral

Age 10 years
Strength 40%
Nose Fruity, floral and honeyed with a little smoke
Taste Light, slightly sweet, with malty, toffee notes and a hint of sherry
Cluster D Light, medium-sweet, low or no peat, with fruity, floral, malty notes and nutty hints
Similar to Speyside, Tobermory, Aultmore

TAMNAVULIN

{TAM-*na*-VOO-*lin*}

Tamnavulin is Gaelic for "mill on the hill", as it was built on the site of a former woollen mill in the Glen of Livet. The distillery was completed in 1966 beside the Allt a Choire (Corrie stream), a tributary of the river Livet. It is a very modern distillery with a rather bleak, functional look. The exception is the old mill visitor centre with its water wheel (pictured), described as the "nicest centre on the whisky trail" by the Northern Scot magazine.

It draws its water from underground springs at Easterton and its cooling water from the Allt a Choire. It operates a stainless steel mash tun, 4 large stainless steel washbacks with a capacity of 69,000 litres (121,000 pints) and 6 stills. It is fully computerised and can be run by a small team. The whisky is matured in bourbon American oak and refill casks in modern warehouses at the distillery, where the casks are racked twelve high.

Tamnavulin Single Speyside Malt whisky is available at 12 years old (profiled) and at 24 and 28 years old as the Stillman's Dram. The label states that it is naturally light and is known as the "Queen of Speyside". Other versions are available, such as a 1989 vintage in Gordon & MacPhail's Connoisseurs Choice range, and a 1992 in Cadenhead's Authentic Collection. The whisky is mainly used in Whyte & Mackay, Mackinlay and Crawfords blends.

Tamnavulin distillery has converted the former mill into an attractive visitor centre, also featured on the label of the malt whisky. Visitors are shown a short video film about the making of whisky and given a guided tour of the distillery and tastings. It also has a shop and a picnic area set in spectacular scenery. At the time of writing the distillery and visitor centre were closed, but it is hoped that they will re-open in the near future.

Feature	Profile
●	Body
●●●	Sweetness
●●	Smoky
	Medicinal
	Tobacco
	Honey
●●	Spicy
	Winey
●●	Nutty
●	Malty
●●	Fruity
●●●	Floral

Age 12 years
Strength 40%
Nose Fragrant, grassy and fruity with a whiff of smoke
Taste Light and sweet, coconuts, some citrus fruit, pepper and a light smokiness
Cluster H Medium-bodied, medium-sweet, with smoky, fruity, spicy notes and floral, nutty hints
Similar to Strathmill, Craigellachie, Balblair

NATURALLY LIGHT

TAMNAVULIN
SPEYSIDE

Single Malt
Rare Scotch Whisky

AGED IN OAK CASKS
RICH & MELLOW

DISTILLED, MATURED & BOTTLED IN SCOTLAND

Aged **12** *Years*

PRODUCT OF SCOTLAND

TEANINICH

{TEA-*an-in-ich*}

Teaninich distillery was founded by Captain Hugh Munro in 1817 on his own land, but has lately been overrun by a modern industrial estate as Alness expanded. One of the earliest to be licensed, it initially struggled against illicit competition, but by 1830 had become a thriving business. Alfred Barnard visited it in 1885, when he noted that "the surrounding country is naturally rich and fertile, and we were struck with the beauty of the cornfields, ripe with golden grain". He observed that it was the only distillery north of Inverness to be lit by electricity.

It was extended and refitted in 1899, power being supplied by two water wheels fed from a dam, later supplemented by a steam engine. These continued to be the main source of power until the 1960s, when it was converted to electricity with steam-heated stills. In 1970 a new still house with 6 stills was added, and the milling, mashing and fermentation unit was rebuilt in 1973.

The emblem on the bottle is a porpoise, examples of which can be seen in the Cromarty Firth nearby. Teaninich's process and cooling water is drawn from Dairywell Spring.

The whisky is matured in American bourbon and European sherry casks in warehouses on the site. Most is used for blends such as Dimple, Haig and Vat 69. Teaninich Single Malt (profiled) is available at 10 years old in Diageo's Flora and Fauna range, and as Teaninich 1973 Vintage in the Rare Malts range.

It does not have a visitor centre or offer tours.

Feature	Profile
●●	Body
●●	Sweetness
●●	Smoky
●	Medicinal
	Tobacco
	Honey
●●	Spicy
	Winey
	Nutty
	Malty
●●	Fruity
●●	Floral

Age 10 years
Strength 43%
Nose Fresh, fruity and grassy, with a hint of peat
Taste Aperitif-style malt with citrus, floral and spice notes, and a salty finish
Cluster H Medium-bodied, medium-sweet, with smoky, fruity, spicy notes and floral, nutty hints
Similar to Glenmorangie, Balblair, Glen Garioch

HIGHLAND
SINGLE MALT
SCOTCH WHISKY

The *Cromarty Firth* is one of the few places in the British Isles inhabited by *PORPOISE*. They can be seen quite regularly, *swimming* close to the shore *less* than a *mile* from

TEANINICH

distillery. Founded in 1817 in the *Ross–shire* town of ALNESS, the *distillery* is now one of the largest in *Scotland.* TEANINICH is an assertive *single MALT WHISKY* with a *spicy, smoky, satisfying* taste.

AGED **10** YEARS

43% vol   Distilled & Bottled in SCOTLAND
               TEANINICH DISTILLERY,
               Alness, Ross-shire, Scotland   70cl

TOBERMORY

{TOBER-*more-ay*}

Tobermory distillery, was originally established as Ledaig distillery in 1798 by John Sinclair, a local merchant, and was first licensed in 1823. It is set in the attractive fishing village of Tobermory, at the northern tip of the island of Mull. The island is steeped in history, home of the Lord of the Isles at Aros Castle, now a ruin, and the ancestral seat of Clan Maclaren at Castle Duart. About 400 yards from the pier lies the Spanish galleon *San Juan de Sicilia,* which exploded in 1588, laden with doubloons.

The distillery had a chequered history, in and out of ownership, sometimes operating but frequently silent. It produces a heavily peated malt whisky called Ledaig (pronounced "led-chig" Gaelic for safe haven), whereas Tobermory (Gaelic for Mary's Well) is reserved for an un-peated expression, though a whiff of smoke is evident from the water.

It draws its water from a private lochen set on the hill above the distillery and uses unpeated malted barley for its principal Tobermory malt whisky. The distillery was substantially upgraded in the 1990s and is now capable of producing a million litres of spirit a year.

It operates a traditional copper-domed cast-iron mash tun, 4 Oregon pine washbacks and 4 medium-sized stills fitted with unique very steep S-shaped lyne arms giving heavy reflux. The whisky is matured in a mixture of ex-bourbon American oak and ex-sherry European oak casks.

Tobermory Single Malt whisky is available at 10 years old (profiled), and in special editions such as a 32 years old cask-strength version finished in oloroso sherry casks. The heavily peated Ledaig Single Malt is available at 7 and 10 years old and in a single cask sherry

Feature	Profile
●	Body
●	Sweetness
●	Smoky
	Medicinal
	Tobacco
●	Honey
	Spicy
	Winey
●	Nutty
● ●	Malty
● ●	Fruity
● ●	Floral

Age 10 years
Strength 40%
Nose Delicately aromatic and malty, with a whiff of smoke
Taste Light, medium dry with fruit and floral notes, and hints of walnuts and honey
Cluster D Light, medium-sweet, low or no peat, with fruity, floral, malty notes and nutty hints
Similar to Aultmore, Tamdhu, Speyside

finish edition. Ledaig is classified in cluster J, and the contrast between the two malts is so marked as to demonstrate the fallacy of 'regional' styles. The malts are used in Scottish Leader, Black Bottle and other Scotch whisky blends.

Tobermory visitor centre and shop are open all year. It offers a video about the history of Tobermory, guided tours and tastings.

TOMATIN

{*tom*-AH-*tin*}

Tomatin is Gaelic for "hill of the juniper bushes", which describes its pretty setting in the Monadhliath mountains. The history of Tomatin can be traced back to the 15th century, when drovers would pause here on their journey to market to fill up their whisky flasks from a still alongside the Old Laird's House. At 1,030 feet (315 metres) above sea level, it is one of the highest distilleries in Scotland. It was built during the Victorian boom of 1897 and expanded from its original 2 stills to 23 stills by 1974. It was then Scotland's largest malt whisky distillery, capable of producing 13 million litres (7½ million pints) of alcohol a year, but this is no longer the case since some of the stills have been removed. The buildings are mostly of industrial design, although some from the original distillery have been retained, including a nineteenth-century dunnage warehouse with blackened stone walls and an earth floor.

The distillery's water flows over the quartz and granite of the Monadhliath mountains, through peat bogs and heather into the Allt-na-Frithe (the "free burn"). It operates a semi-Lauter stainless steel mash tun, 12 stainless steel washbacks and 12 small pot stills; the others have been de-commissioned. The stills have boil balls incorporated in the necks, with a pinched waist, to encourage reflux. Tomatin also has its own cooperage, where casks are built and maintained by coopers. At 65,000 litres (14,300 gallons) of spirit per week, it is one of the largest producers of malt whisky in Scotland. Tomatin whisky is mostly matured in ex-bourbon American oak casks, with a few sherry butts to give a sherried note to the malts.

Tomatin Single Highland Malt whisky is available at 12 years old (profiled), and at 25 years old non chill-filtered. The company also produces several blends, including Talisman, 5 years old

Feature	Profile
●●	Body
●●●	Sweetness
●●	Smoky
	Medicinal
	Tobacco
●●	Honey
●●	Spicy
●	Winey
●	Nutty
●●	Malty
	Fruity
●	Floral

Age 12 years
Strength 40%
Nose Aromatic and sweet, with malt and light smoke notes
Taste Apples, honey and spice. A long nutty, liquorice finish and a hint of sherry
Cluster F Medium-bodied, medium-sweet, low peat, malty notes and sherry, honey, spicy hints
Similar to Ardmore, Fettercairn, Glen Deveron

"Big T", and two Antiquary deluxe blends aged 12 and 21 years old.

The visitor centre and shop are open all year round. The centre offers a short video film, tours and tastings.

TOMINTOUL

*{tom-in-*TOWEL}

Tomintoul is a modern distillery built in 1965 and extended in 1974. Its functional, industrial buildings are situated in the beautifully wooded valley of Avonside near Tomintoul, the highest village in Scotland.

It draws its water from Ballantruan Spring and its malted barley is delivered lightly peated to order. It operates a large semi-Lauter mash tun, 6 stainless steel washbacks and 4 tall stills incorporating boil balls in the neck to increase reflux. The size of the stills and the use of boil balls account for the lightness of the resulting spirit. It also has a blending unit where trade customers can create their own vatted malts or blended whiskies to order. The whisky is matured in a mixture of ex-bourbon American oak casks, refill hogsheads and a few oloroso sherry oak butts, hence its lightly sherried note to the malts. The bulk of the production goes for blending, notably in Whyte & Mackay blends, and for use in 'own label' brands. If you buy a supermarket Speyside Single Malt, there is a good chance it is from Tomintoul.

Tomintoul Single Speyside Malt whisky is available at 10 years old

Feature	Profile
	Body
●●●	Sweetness
●	Smoky
	Medicinal
	Tobacco
●●	Honey
●●	Spicy
●	Winey
●	Nutty
●●	Malty
●	Fruity
●●	Floral

Age 10 years
Strength 40%
Nose Light, fragrant and grassy, with a malty edge
Taste Quite sweet with oaky vanilla and spice notes, and hints of citrus fruits and sherry
Cluster E Light, medium-sweet, low peat, with floral, malty notes and fruity, spicy, honey hints
Similar to Inchgower, Glenallachie, Loch Lomond

(profiled), at 16 years old, and at 27 years old. The distillery has been maturing a peaty version for several years, unusual for a Speyside distillery, and this will confound the pundits who insist on attributing regional 'styles' to malt whiskies.

Although the distillery does not have a visitor centre or shop, visitors are welcome by appointment.

40% vol

TORMORE

{*tor*-MORE}

Tormore distillery was designed in 1958 by the architect Sir Albert Richardson, a past president of the Royal Academy better known for restoring Georgian mansions. It is set on a slope with panoramic views over Speyside and the Cromdale Hills. The main production buildings are arranged around a square courtyard, fronted by an ornamental lake with fountains, flanked by gardens and topiary stills. In winter the fountain was removed and the lake used as a curling rink. In the belfry to the right is an unusual clock that chimes "Highland Laddie" on the hour, followed by "Coming through the Rye", "Corn Rigs" and "Bonnie Lass of Fyvie" at the quarter-hours. The manager's house to the left and workers' houses at the rear are white-harled with margined windows and doors. Built for Long John Distillers as a showcase distillery during the 1950s, it is styled the "Pearl of Speyside" because of its dramatic architecture at the start of the Speyside Whisky Trail.

It draws its soft water from Achvochkie Burn, which flows down granite hills and through peat and heather, rising cold and crystal clear above the distillery. It operates a large stainless steel Lauter mash tun, 8 stainless steel washbacks and 8 relatively large stills. The whisky is matured in refill casks, mostly American oak, stored in 6 warehouses behind the distillery.

Tormore Single Speyside Malt whisky is available at 12 years old (profiled), and at 15 years old through Gordon and MacPhail and other independents. Most of its production is used in blends such as Ballantine's, Teachers, Long John and Stewart's Cream of the Barley.

It is a pity the distillery does not have a visitor centre, for its twentieth-century architectural design is unique and was intended as a showcase. Visitors are welcome by appointment, however, and open days are occasionally organised through the Moray Society.

Feature	Profile
●●	Body
●●	Sweetness
●	Smoky
	Medicinal
	Tobacco
●	Honey
	Spicy
●	Winey
●●	Nutty
●	Malty
	Fruity
	Floral

Age 12 years
Strength 40%
Nose Light and nutty, with hints of honey and sherry
Taste Slightly sweet, malty with a whiff of smoke
Cluster F Medium-bodied, medium-sweet, low peat, malty notes and sherry, honey, spicy hints
Similar to Ardmore, Glenrothes, Auchroisk

TULLIBARDINE

{*tully*-BAR-*deen*}

Tullibardine distillery nestles at the foor of the Ochil Hills in Blackford, Perthshire at the gateway to the Scottish Highlands. It is named after Tullibardine Moor, now famous as the estate of Gleneagles Hotel and its champion golf courses. Its soft clear water is drawn from Danny Burn, the same source that supplied the first public brewery in Scotland from which King James IV purchased beer for his coronation at Scone in 1488 – hence Tullibardine's excellent new visitor centre is named "1488" and its whisky is styled "The Majestic Malt". The water is also historically infamous. Legend has it that the 12th century Norwegian King Magnus lost his wife Helen while attempting to cross the River Allan nearby. The drowned queen was buried at the scene and her grave is visible at Deaf Knowe near the ford, and thus the village was named "Black Ford". Two brands of Scottish mineral mater are bottled from the same source – Highland Spring and Gleneagles. The first Tullibardine distillery was established by William and Henry Bannerman in 1798 at a farm near Blackford, but it ceased operating in 1837. The former brewery was converted to the present distillery by the architect William Delmé Evans in 1949, and was rebuilt in 1973. It operates a stainless steel mash tun, 6 stainless steel washbacks and four stills. The whiskies are mostly matured in American oak barrels, some of which have been seasoned with sherry, and are stored in dunnage warehouses at the site.

Tullibardine Single Highland Malt whisky is available as a selected vintage, currently 1993 (profiled), and at various single cask bottlings, including a rare 1965 vintage, and a 1986 Manager's Dram sheery hogshead. Special wine finishes include port, muscatel and marsala, the port edition being surprisingly pink.

Another unique product is Tullibardine's 1488 Whisky Ale. Distillery wort is sent to Bridge of Allen brewery for brewing into ale, which is then matured for around 15 weeks in ex-whisky casks.

The distillery's excellent "1488" visitor centre offers tours tastings, dining and shopping. There is a distillery shop, a 1488 café serving hot and cold meals and other retail outlets. It's a great place to stop for lunch when heading north to Perth.

Feature	Profile
●●	Body
●●●	Sweetness
	Smoky
	Medicinal
●	Tobacco
	Honey
●●	Spicy
●	Winey
●	Nutty
●●	Malty
●●	Fruity
●	Floral

Age 12 years
Strength 40%
Nose Fragrant, sweet and malty with zesty citric notes
Taste Creamy texture with some spice, hints of vanilla and nuts, and a fruity finish
Cluster F Medium-bodied, medium-sweet, low peat, malty notes and sherry, honey, spicy hints
Similar to Glen Keith, Glenrothes, Auchroisk

GLENGYLE

Glengyle distillery was built in 1872 by William Mitchell, a Campbeltown farmer who had previously owned Springbank distillery with his brother John since 1837 until they parted following a quarrel over sheep.

In 1876 Alfred Barnard described it as "neat and compact, spacious and clean, with a fine view of cultured gardens, cultivated fields, and hill slopes covered with heather". He would not be disappointed today, though the views have changed as Campbeltown has expanded. But it was in a sorry state in 2000, having been used for other business for 75 years, when the owners of Springbank distillery bought it again and began restoring its Victorian buildings. This was sensitively completed in 2004, with 2 small stills removed from Ben Wyvis and reconditioned, a malt mill from Craigellachie, 4 large boat-skin washbacks built at the site and a new mash tun installed.

Its water is drawn from Crosshill Loch, fed by springs on Beinn Ghuilean, and it uses ligthly peated malted barley supplied from the traditional floor maltings at Springbank. The whisky is double distilled, and matured in a mixture of casks of which around half are American oak ex-bourbon hogsheads, the balance being sherry, port, Madeira and refill casks.

The whiskies will be bottled as Kilkerran Single Campbeltown Malt whisky. "Kilkerran" is derived from the Gaelic "Ceann Loch Cille Chiarain", the name of the original settlement at Campbeltown, believed to have been founded by the 6th century Irish monk St Ciarán or Kieran. This lends support to the theory that whisky was brounght to Scotland by Irish missionary monks. Glengyle was officially opened in March 2004, the first new distillery in Campbeltown for over 125 years. Although the single malt will not be available for some time, you can purchase bottles from the first distillation, matured in six different wood types, and the company will send you a progress sample at 5 years old.

It does not have a visitor centre, but tours can be arranged in the summer by appointment. There is a shop, Eaglesome, in Campbeltown and you can get more information and order the whisky at *kilkerran.com*.

KILCHOMAN

In the nineteenth century there were many farm distilleries on Islay, but they were all overtaken or absorbed by the commercial producers. Kilchoman is Scotland's newest distillery, the dream of its founder Anthony Wills to re-create a farm distillery much as it would have been 150 years ago.

It was completed in 2005, the first distillery to be built on Islay for 125 years. Its location at Rockside Farm on the west coast of Islay beside Machir Bay is spectacular, an area steeped in history as evidenced by a 14th century cross in the church graveyard nearby.

Kilchoman is a charming boutique distillery with traditional maltings, a single pagoda chimney and the smallest stills allowed by law. Production levels are tiny at 80,000 litres of alcohol a year, or about 650 casks, the smallest in Scotland.

The barley, grown in the surrounding fields, is first steeped in water, then turned by hand on the malting floor to germinate, and dried in a kiln over a peat fire. The aim is to produce a fairly heavily peated whisky of the traditional Islay style. It operates a stainless steel mash tun, two stainless steel washbacks and two tiny swan-necked stills heated by steam. The wash still has a boil ball in the neck, to increase reflux and lighten the spirit.

The whisky is matured in American ex-bourbon oak barrels and refill casks, with a few sherry butts reserved for special expressions. The first Kilchoman single malt should become available in 2010, and you can reserve a cask in advance.

Visitors to Kilchoman are most definitely welcome. You can see, and participate in, the complete whisky making process, from sowing and reaping the barley, through all the stages of production, to bottling the single malt. Book ahead to stay at the farm and get totally involved in the work. It has a fine visitor centre with an exhibition on the history of farm distilling on Islay, a shop and a café. If you cannot manage to get there in person, go to *kilchomandistillery.com*.

FLAVOUR VOCABULARY

1. BODY/WEIGHT

light, light-to-medium, medium, medium-to-full, big, bold, delicate, dense, firm, full, heavy, powerful, robust, round, weighty

2. SWEETNESS

astringent, dry, medium, medium-dry, medium-sweet, sweet

3. PEATY/SMOKY

Smoky ash, bonfires, brimstone, burnt-sticks, cinnamon-sticks-burning, coal-gas, cordite, creosote, guaiacol, heather-peat, heather-smoke, heathery-burnt, incense, Lapsang-Souchong tea, matchboxes, molasses, oilskins, peat-reek, peaty, phenolic, pungent, rubbery, smoke-exotic, smoky, sooty, spent-fireworks, steam-engines, tar, tarred-rope, turf-burning

Kippery anchovies, dried-crab-shells, dried-shellfish, kippery sea-shells, shellfish-dried, shells-dried-crab, smoked-mussels, smoked-oysters, smoked-salmon

Mossy bracken, earthy, fishing-nets, moss-water, peat-fresh, roots, turf-fresh.

4. MEDICINAL/SALTY

Medicinal antiseptic, bath-salts, beachy, brine, Brylcreem, carbolic, diesel-oil, eucalyptus, germoline, hospitals, iodine, iron, kelp, lint, menthol, neoprene, salty, oysters ozone, sea-air, seashore, sea-spray, seaweed, surgical-spirits, TCP, turpentine

5. TOBACCO/FEINTY

Tobacco tea-chests, teapots, tobacco-aromatic, tobacco-ash, tobacco-stale

Feinty acetic, blotting-paper, bung-cloth, cardboard, cork, damp-wool,

fusty, inky, metallic, mothballs, mouldy, musty, musty-oak, old-books, paraffin, vinegar, wood-old

Leathery calf-book-binding, car-seats, cowhide, libraries, poultry-food, saddles

Sweaty buttermilk, cheesy, drains, gym-shoes-old, leather-polish, musky, piggery, shoe-polish, sickly, stale, waxed-raincoats

Plastic oilskins, plastic-buckets, plastic-mats, scorched-plastic

6. HONEY/VANILLA

Honey beeswax, honey-clover, honey-heather, honey-lavender, honey-pouring, mead

Vanilla butterscotch, cake-mix, candy-floss, caramel, cocoa-butter, cola, custard-powder, fudge, glycerine, rum-toffee, sticky-toffee-pudding, syrupy, tablet, toffee, treacle

7. SPICY/WOODY

Spicy allspice, caraway, cedar, cedarwood, chicken-masala, chilli-peppers, cigar-boxes, cinnamon, cloves, ginger, gingerbread, mustard, mustard-cress, newly-sharpened-pencils, nutmeg, oaky, pepper, pine, resinous, sandalwood, sawdust, tannic, wood-new, woody

8. WINEY/SHERRY

Sherried bourbon, brandy, burgundy, calvados, chardonnay, cider-apples, drinks-cabinet, ethereal, fino-sherry, grapey, grappa, liqueurish, madeira, manzanilla, oloroso, port, rum, sherry, spirituous, spirity, vinous, winey

9. NUTTY/CREAMY

Nutty almonds, benzaldehyde, brazil-nuts, candlewax, filbert, gun-oil, hazelnuts, lanolin, linseed-oil, marzipan, oily, olives, praline, rapeseed-oil, roasted-peanuts, unctuous, walnuts

Creamy butter, chocolate, coconuts, hand-cream, milk-chocolate, silky

10. MALTY/CEREAL

Cooked Mash agricultural, barley, biscuits, cereal-mash, draff, grain, mealy, oats, porridge, silage-sweet, Weetabix

Cooked Veg corn-boiled, potato-mashed, potato-skins-baked, swede-cooked, turnips-cooked

Malty hops, Horlicks, malt-extract, malted-milk, Marmite,

Husky bran, chaff, hops-dried, iron-tonic, pot-ale

Toasted aniseed, biscuits-digestive, bitter-chocolate, bitter-coffee, burnt, burnt-cake, burnt-toast, burnt-toffee, cocoa, cake, coffee-grounds, coffee-roasted, cookies, hickory, liquorice, roasted-malt, shortbread

Yeasty baking, baking-bread, fleshy, gralloch, gravy, meaty, pork-boiled, roast-meat, sausages, venison

11. FRUITY/ESTERY

Citric ascorbic, bergamot, estery, Kiwi-fruit, lemon-sherbet, lemons, limes, mandarins, orange-rind, oranges, peel-zest, pineapple-cubes, tangerines, tart, tropical-fruit

Fresh Fruit apples, autumn-fruits, bananas, blackberries, cherries, custard-pudding, fresh-figs, fruit-green, fruit-gums, fruity, green-fruit, humbugs, lemonade, melons, peaches, pear-drops, pears, pineapples, raspberries, strawberries, sweet-shop

Cooked Fruit baked-apples, banana-rum, fruit-cooked, fruit-rotten, marmalade, plummy, prunes-stewed, raspberry-jam, stewed-apples, stewed-rhubarb

Dried Fruit apricots-dried, candy-peel, Christmas-cake, Christmas-pudding, dates, Dundee-cake, figs-dried, fruit-cake, mince-pies, peel-mixed, prunes, raisins, sultanas

Solvent American-cream-soda, bubble-gum, cellophane, ethyl-alcohol, fusil-oil, nail-varnish-remover, paint-fresh, pine-essence

12. FLORAL/HERBAL

Fragrant acetal, aromatic, barber-shop, blossom, bluebells, Earl-Grey-tea, elderflowers, floral, flowery, freesias, gentian-roses, gorse-bushes, heather, honeysuckle, lavender, lilac, marc, orange-blossom, orchards, perfumed, quinine, rhododendrons, roses, rose-water, scented, summer, violets, wet-spring-mornings

Greenhouse apple-mint, barley-sugar, bog-myrtle, boiled-sweets, carnations, flowering-currants, geraniums, green-tomatoes, mint, peppermint, sherbet, spearmint, sugared-almonds

Leafy aldehydic, coffee-green, cut-barley, cut-grass, fresh, fir-trees,green-apples, green-sticks, green-vegetables, greeny, laurel-leaves, lawn-cuttings, pea-pods, pine-cones, sappy

Herbal artichokes, barns, bayleaf, botanical, coumarin, dry-hay, fennel, grassy, green-hedgerows, harvest-fields, hay, hay-damp, heather-flowers, heathery, meadows, mulch, oregano, sage-and-onion, soap-saddle, soap-scented, straw, tea thyme

INDEX

ACKNOWLEDGEMENTS

The following have been especially helpful in giving advice and encouragement: Crescens Akkermans, Bobby Anderson, Pamela van Ankeren, Raymond Armstrong, Helen Arthur, Elaine Bailey, Rachel Barrie, Michael Beamish, William Bergius, Valerie Blanc, Neil Boyd, John and Sue Broome, Amanda Brown, Neil Cameron, Jane Catternach, George Christie, David Cox, Ronnie Cox, Douglas Cruikshank, Bob Dalgarno, Tracy Davidson, Ed Dodson, David Doig, Gavin Durnin, Ella Edgar, Graham Eunson, Marion Ferguson, Robert Fleming, George Forsyth, John L. S. Grant, Alan Greig, Glen Gribbon, Michael Haig, Michael Heads, Iain Henderson, Darren Hosie, Richard Joynson, Gillian Kelso, David King, John Lamond, Ronnie Learmond, Jim Long, René Looper, Bill Lumsden, Tom McCulloch, Jim McEwan, Des McGacherty, Frank McHardy, Charles MacLean, Ian MacMillan, Dennis Malcolm, Ian Millar, Douglas Milne, Wallace Milroy, Euan Mitchell, Gordon Motion, Betty Munro, Norma Munro, Hans Offringa, Jockie Paterson, Richard Paterson, Annie Pugh, John Ramsay, Mark Reynier, Graeme Richardson, Fiona Richardson, Alastair Robertson, Allan and Isla Robertson, David Robertson, Colin Ross, Douglas Ross, Ronnie Routledge, Lorna Sheriff, Andrew Sinclair, Derek Sinclair, Stuart Smith, David Stewart, Keir Sword, Andrew Symington, William Tait, Yvonne Thackeray, Jackie and Stuart Thomson, Margaret Mary Timpson, David Urquhart, Iam Urquhart, Alastair Walker, Gillian Wallace, Wouter Wapenaar, Anthony Wells, Iain Weir, David Whittaker-Smith, Alan Winchester and Vanessa Wright.

Thanks also to those distillers and producers who have generously supported *Whisky Classified* seminars and tutored tastings.

I would also like to acknowledge the assistance of Allied Distillers Ltd, Angus Dundee Distillers Plc, Bacardi & Co. Ltd, Ben Nevis Distillery Ltd, BenRiach Distillery Co. Ltd, Berry Bros & Rudd Ltd, Bruichladdich Distillery Co. Ltd, Burn Stewart Distillers Plc, Chivas Bros. Ltd, Cutty Sark International, Diageo Plc, Delhaize "Le Lion" s.a., John Dewar & Sons Ltd, The Edrington Group, Gall & Gall, Glenmorangie Plc, Gordon & MacPhail Ltd, J & G Grant, William Grant and Sons Ltd, Highland Distillers Ltd, Ian Macleod & Co. Ltd, Isle of Arran Distillers Ltd, Inver House Distillers, Loch Lomond Distillery Co. Ltd, J & A Mitchell & Co. Ltd, Morrison Bowmore Distillers Ltd, Pernod Ricard, Royal Mile Whiskies, Scotch Whisky Association, Signatory Vintage Scotch Whisky Ltd, Speyside Distillery Co. Ltd, Tomatin Distillery Co. Ltd, Uitgeverij Het Spectrum and Whyte & Mackay Ltd.

Lastly, I would like to thank my Publisher, Kate Oldfield; my Designer, Bernard Higton; my Editor, Kate Burkhalter; Photographer, Douglas Robertson; University Press Officer, Gayle Cook; the man who set me up for this, Colin Webb; and my wife Doreen Wishart, for all the help and support she has given to me over the past 10 years.

WHISKY ANALYST

Readers of *Whisky Classified* have frequently asked whether the flavour classification developed in this book can be applied to other single malts not covered here, such as rare and aged expressions, independent bottlings, and new releases. This is now possible with "Whisky Analyst", a computer system designed to find the style and flavour type of a new whisky and to classify it with other similar malts. It is equivalent to the scientific matching of DNA profiles, using sensory data on single malt whiskies.

You simply enter the flavour profile of a new malt whisky into Whisky Analyst's dialogue (below) by coding the intensity of each of the 12 flavour categories. More than 240 million different flavour profiles are possible in this system. Whisky Analyst searches its databank to match the profile you

entered with the ten malt whisky clusters in this book, to find the one that fits it best; then within that cluster it identifies the other malt whiskies that are most similar to it.

With Whisky Analyst, you become the Maltmaster. You can use it to plan a malt whisky tasting, even to design a new malt style. Some skill is required, however, to code a flavour profile correctly for a new whisky, and the following notes may be of help.

Colour Begin by observing the colour of the whisky through a clear glass. Although colour is not a flavour category, it may reveal clues to the whisky's provenance and type. A light colour usually indicates a young whisky, or one that has been matured in un-sherried refill casks, and its flavour should more truly reflect the original spirit. A darker colour can indicate the

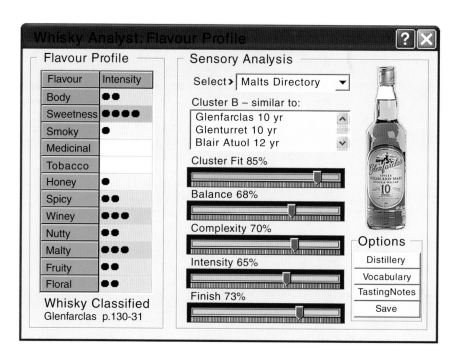

WHISKY ANALYST

influence of sherry wood maturation, and hence wood flavours may dominate; but this is not certain because some producers add spirit caramel to darken lightly coloured whiskies.

Legs Swirl the whisky around the glass and you will notice that it sticks to the side when you place the glass upright – the striping that results is the "legs" of the whisky. Slow legs indicates a sticky, full-bodied whisky, usually associated with age or new-fill cask maturation; lighter whiskies have faster legs.

Nose If you are profiling more than one whisky, try nosing all your whiskies before tasting any of them. Jot down all the scents you find and record their intensities. Some malts have a dominant aroma which is their signature. Try to get behind any strong flavours to find the more subtle ones in the background. Your nose is your best organ for doing this, so allow it plenty of time. The flavours are often complex and multi-layered. Professional maltmasters usually rely solely on the nose when choosing whiskies for malts or blends.

Diluted Taste It is generally easier to taste whiskies that have first been diluted with soft mineral water at room temperature. Do not add ice or chilled water. Try to reduce the strength to about 20% alcohol by volume, paying attention to the strength stated on the label. Whisky Analyst has a guide to the quantity of soft water to be added. Start tasting the lightest floral whiskies first, recording the flavours you detect

Left: *Entering a profile into Whisky Analyst.*

Below: *Nosing a new whisky to check the flavours.*

and their intensity, progressing to the full, sherried, winey or peated ones at the end. You are trying here to identify the flavours of other foods, drinks and aromas that correspond to the flavour of the whisky. Jot down all that you find, and compare your findings with friends if possible. Quite separately, when you are tasting food and drink try to relate them to malt whiskies that are familiar.

Undiluted taste The whiskies can now be tasted at full strength. Hold each

whisky in the mouth for a few seconds, chewing on it to dilute it with saliva, and note the flavours you detect. A very fine Maltmaster friend of mine recommends chewing an undiluted whisky for one second for each year of its age; thus a 30 year old malt should be chewed for half a minute before being swallowed. This may be difficult, but it is essential if you are to detect the subtle flavours masked by any dominant ones.

Below: *Save your results for future reference.*

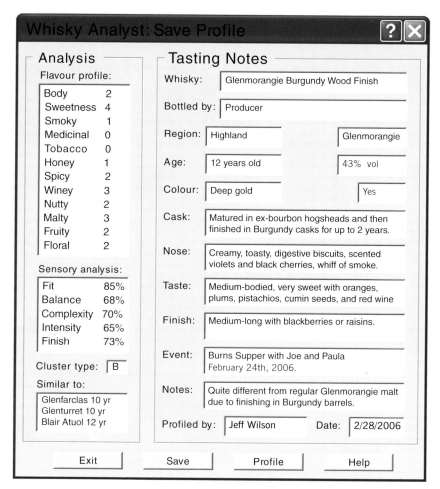

Whisky Analyst: Save Profile   ? ✕

Analysis

Flavour profile:

Body	2
Sweetness	4
Smoky	1
Medicinal	0
Tobacco	0
Honey	1
Spicy	2
Winey	3
Nutty	2
Malty	3
Fruity	2
Floral	2

Sensory analysis:

Fit	85%
Balance	68%
Complexity	70%
Intensity	65%
Finish	73%

Cluster type: B

Similar to:

Glenfarclas 10 yr
Glenturret 10 yr
Blair Atuol 12 yr

Tasting Notes

Whisky:	Glenmorangie Burgundy Wood Finish	
Bottled by:	Producer	
Region:	Highland	Glenmorangie
Age:	12 years old	43% vol
Colour:	Deep gold	Yes
Cask:	Matured in ex-bourbon hogsheads and then finished in Burgundy casks for up to 2 years.	
Nose:	Creamy, toasty, digestive biscuits, scented violets and black cherries, whiff of smoke.	
Taste:	Medium-bodied, very sweet with oranges, plums, pistachios, cumin seeds, and red wine	
Finish:	Medium-long with blackberries or raisins.	
Event:	Burns Supper with Joe and Paula February 24th, 2006.	
Notes:	Quite different from regular Glenmorangie malt due to finishing in Burgundy barrels.	
Profiled by:	Jeff Wilson	Date: 2/28/2006

Exit   Save   Profile   Help

Finish Lastly, record the flavours you find when you swallow the whisky. Does the flavour linger in your mouth after the whisky is swallowed (a long finish) or disappear quite quickly (a short finish)? Can you still taste the whisky later, or the following morning? Try leaving some in the glass and return to it periodically to check the flavours. Think laterally – you may have already found the main flavours, but what else is there in the background?

Compare your notes with your friends, and any other published tasting notes on the bottle, in books, or from the internet. Many good tasting notes can be found on the websites of fine whisky retailers, such as Royal Mile Whiskies, Whisky Exchange and Oddbins, and at Whisky Magazine or Malt Advocate.

Using *Whisky Classified*'s flavour vocabulary, associate the flavours you find with each of the 12 flavour categories, and judge their intensities – are they hints (1), medium notes (2), definite flavours (3), or dominant, full flavours (4)? Rate each flavour accordingly and enter them into your Whisky Analyst flavour profile. It will search for the best whisky cluster into which your whisky is classified, and estimate how good a fit it is. If you have profiled a completely different combination of flavours unlike any other whisky in the classification, which is not possible, the program will tell you this has happened. Whisky Analyst will also tell you which other malt whiskies most closely match the flavour profile entered. You may feel you disagree with the results,

which can easily happen if you have rated the intensities too high or too low. Use this information to review your flavour profile. It will also tell you the most dissimilar single malts, for reference.

When you are satisfied that the flavour profile you have entered is reasonably correct, save it in Whisky Analyst's data bank. Remember to add your own tasting notes, and the other information you have about the whisky, such as its strength, cask type and whether it is chill-filtered, for future reference.

Whisky Analyst can be obtained at *whiskyclassified.com*. It includes a databank of many single malt whiskies that have been profiled by a wide range of contributors, far wider than is possible in this book, and an extended flavour vocabulary. You can submit your own new profiles to *whiskyclassified.com* for addition to the reference set. The ultimate goal is to record a flavour profile for every malt whisky that has been bottled, so that future enthusiasts will have a scientific and objective source to which they can refer.

The scientific method used in this book, and in Whisky Analyst, to classify single malt whiskies is well established. David Wishart has a doctorate in classification theory and has developed Clustan, a computer system for cluster analysis that is used widely in the social and biological sciences. The clustering method has also been published by Dr Wishart in an *Encyclopedia of Behavioural Statistics*, Wiley, 2005.